Success Strategies From Heaven

by
Keith Butler

Success Strategies From Heaven

by
Keith Butler

HARRISON HOUSE
Tulsa, Oklahoma

Success Strategies From Heaven
ISBN 0-89274-745-5
Copyright © 1995 by Keith Butler
P. O. Box 34546
Detroit, Michigan 48234

Published by Harrison House, Inc.
P. O. Box 35035
Tulsa, Oklahoma 74153

Contents

Introduction

Let me ask you this question: Has there ever been a time in your life when you have *never* stumbled or failed, or *never* made a mistake?

I think your answer is obvious. At some point in our lives we all have stumbled or failed. We all have made mistakes and paid the price as a result.

The important thing to realize, though, is you don't always have to be stumbling or falling.

Would you like to know how to *never* stumble or fall? I believe you will learn how as you carefully read the pages of this book.

What does the word *never* mean? Its definition is simple: *Never* means never — not ever at any time! In other words, it just will not happen.

In this study you will learn from God's Word how you can avoid some pitfalls in your life.

Never stumble or fall is a phrase taken from the apostle Peter's writings to the Church. This is a goal we can shoot for: to be in the position where we *never* stumble or fall. That's what Peter was talking about.

I had read this portion of Scripture probably hundreds, maybe thousands, of times. I had preached it many times. But then as I was reading it again, I saw it in a way I had not seen it before: how we are to *never* stumble or fall.

When it dawned on me that there was something available in the Word of God to teach me how to never stumble or fall, I thought, *I had better look at this again.* When

I did, the Holy Spirit began to show me this truth from God's Word.

As I share with you through the following pages, I pray the Holy Spirit will open your understanding to this truth, as He did mine.

1
You Shall Never Fall!

Our foundation text in this study is taken from the Second Epistle of Peter, chapter 1. Let's look first at verse 10:

> Wherefore the rather, brethren, give diligence to make your calling and election sure: for if ye do these things, ye shall *never fall* [or fail].

In *The Amplified Bible* the latter part of this verse says:

> ...make steadfast your calling and election; for if you do this you will *never stumble or fall*.

In this epistle Peter was teaching God's people how to *never* stumble or fall. He gave them some instructions and then said, "If you take heed to these things — if you do these things — you shall *never* fall!"

This is a goal we can reach for. We need to know the things we can do that will cause us to *never* stumble, to *never* fall. The answers are found right here in this chapter of God's Word.

Look closer at this portion of Scripture and read the verses leading up to verse 10. This gives us some idea, some clue, of how it is that we will never stumble or fall.

"Like Precious Faith"

Let's begin at the beginning:

> Simon Peter, a servant and an apostle [or special messenger] of Jesus Christ, to them that have obtained

like precious faith with us through the righteousness of God and of our Saviour Jesus Christ.

2 Peter 1:1

From this verse we know that, as believers in the Lord Jesus Christ, we have received **like precious faith** through Him. We have been given the faith of God.

"Grace"

Grace...be multiplied unto you through the knowledge of God, and of Jesus our Lord.

2 Peter 1:2

Verse 2 in *The Amplified Bible* says:

May *grace (God's favor)*...be multiplied to you in (the full, personal, precise and correct) knowledge of God and of Jesus our Lord.

I want you to understand what Peter was saying here: **May grace (God's favor)...be multiplied to you.** He was praying for those believers and saying to them, "May God's favor be yours."

We know then that grace means God's favor. Favor allows us to do things that others cannot do. Let me give you an example.

I have favor in my parent's house. I have been given liberty there. I can unlock the door, walk straight to the kitchen, open the refrigerator and help myself to whatever I find to eat. I can do that without any fear of getting a 12-gauge shotgun blast in my back.

But suppose a stranger sneaked into my parent's house. If he opened the refrigerator and started fumbling around for some food, he might be surprised at the result. He will never receive the same kind of favor that I receive.

That's what favor is.

When God gives us favor, we are really blessed! With godly favor, we receive favor from both God and man. Then comes peace.

"Peace"

Let's look at verse 2 again from *The Amplified Bible*. Besides grace, Peter was praying that the Church know God's peace. The description of peace is given in this verse:

> **May grace (God's favor) and** *peace,* **(which is perfect well-being, all necessary good, all spiritual prosperity and freedom from fears and agitating passions and moral conflicts) be multiplied to you.**

We see here that peace has a sixfold definition: perfect well-being, all necessary good, all spiritual prosperity, freedom from fear, deliverance from agitating passions and deliverance from all moral conflicts.

Included in this peace is the freedom from fear — *all* fear.

Think of all the fears you could be experiencing these days: fear of crime, fear of failure, fear of sickness and disease, fear of financial loss, fear of dying young, fear of losing your loved ones, fear that something bad will happen to you.

This one verse covers any area of fear you can imagine.

Peter was praying that God's people be set free from *all* fears. He wanted them to be free from agitating passions — passions of the flesh, things the body craves and desires. He wanted them to be free from moral conflicts. When you are without those conflicts, you can know God's way and be able to function and operate in it.

"Knowledge"

In verse 2 Peter was pronouncing a blessing upon God's people. Let's look at it again:

> **Grace and peace be multiplied unto you through the** *knowledge* **of God, and of Jesus our Lord** (KJV).

> **May grace (God's favor) and peace...be multiplied to you in (the full, personal, precise and correct)** *knowledge* **of God and of Jesus our Lord** (AMP).

We know the New Testament was written originally in Greek, and there are several Greek renderings for the word *knowledge.* We will look at two Greek words found in this chapter.

The Greek word in verse 2 translated "knowledge" is *epignosis,* which means a full and exact knowledge.[1]

The key here is gaining *epignosis* — that full, complete and exact knowledge of God; coming to know His character, what He has done for you, what He has put in you. The more you learn about God and Jesus, the more you will be kept from stumbling or falling.

The apostle Peter prayed that the Church might have the full, complete, exact knowledge of God and of the Lord Jesus Christ. He prayed that because he knew knowledge was the key to victory.

You need to realize that *epignosis* — exact knowledge — is the key to victory in *your* life, too.

Peter was saying to the Church: "In order for you to neither stumble nor fall, you need to have the *epignosis* — the full, complete, exact knowledge of God and of Jesus our Lord."

"All Things That Pertain Unto Life and Godliness"

Continuing in this passage of Scripture, we read:

> According as his divine power hath given unto us *all things* that pertain unto life and godliness.
>
> **2 Peter 1:3**

In *The Amplified Bible* this verse says:

> For His divine power has bestowed upon us *all things* that [are requisite and suited] to life and godliness.

---

[1]James H. Strong. *Strong's Exhaustive Concordance.* Compact Ed. (Grand Rapids: Baker, 1992), "Greek Dictionary of the New Testament," p. 31, #1922.

In this verse the word *all* is a key. *All* means God has given us everything. It says we have been given *all* **things that pertain unto life and godliness.**

The *New American Standard Bible* says it this way:

...seeing that His divine power has granted to us *everything* **pertaining to life and godliness.**

Through His divine power, God has given us everything so that we might be able to win in this life. He has given us a promise in His Word for enough supernatural ability to bring about victory.

"More Knowledge"

We receive **everything pertaining to life and godliness** through knowledge, but not through knowledge alone. In verse 3 Peter goes on to say:

...through the knowledge of him that hath called us to glory and virtue.

In *The Amplified Bible* it says:

...through the (full, personal) knowledge of Him Who called us by and to His own glory and excellence (virtue).

In the *New American Standard Bible* it says:

...through the true knowledge of Him who called us by His own glory and excellence.

In other words, the more you know and understand the Lord Jesus and have a closer rapport with Him, the easier it will be for you to receive the promises that are available in this life.

God has given *you* a promise in His Word for power through the knowledge of Him so that you will be able to exercise victory in *every* area of your life. That means having victory at home with your spouse. It means raising your children the way God commands in His Word. It means knowing how to handle your financial affairs.

No matter what you may have to deal with in this life, God has provided victory for you in advance. That victory comes through the *epignosis.*

The Greek word for "knowledge" in verse 3 is also *epignosis.* **All things that pertain unto life and godliness** come through the exact, full knowledge of God — His character, Who He is, what He has done for you.

This means having knowledge of God the Father as Jehovah the Lord. You need to know about Jehovah. In the Hebrew He is given several names, such as Jehovah-Jireh, Jehovah-Rapha, Jehovah-Tsidkenu, Jehovah-Nissi. The more knowledge you receive of Him, the more you will be able to walk in His blessing. That's why knowledge is power.

"Escaping the World's Corruption"

Peter goes on in verse 4 to say:

> **Whereby are given unto us exceeding great and precious promises: that by these ye might be partakers of the divine nature,** *having escaped the corruption* **that is in the world through lust.**
>
> **2 Peter 1:4**

As believers, we accept all that Jesus has done for us: He died on the cross, took sin in our place and rose triumphantly from the grave, having defeated the power of sin and Satan. When we receive all He did for us, we become partakers of His divine nature. Then we are able to escape all the corruption that is going on in the world around us.

People are being destroyed throughout the world today. We can see and hear what is happening by watching and listening to news reports.

AIDS has become one of the top news subjects. In one African country, a third of all adults has been infected with the AIDS virus. That means one out of three persons in that country has the virus. As a result, millions of children are being orphaned as their parents are dying of that disease.

AIDS is one way in which the world is being destroyed, and it has come about because of the lust of the flesh.

But God does not intend for His people to be destroyed with the world.

The Amplified Bible says it this way:

By means of these (referring to those promises) He has bestowed on us His precious and exceedingly great promises, so that through them you may escape (by flight) from the moral decay (rottenness and corruption) that is in the world because of covetousness (lust and greed), and become sharers (partakers) of the divine nature.

2 Peter 1:4 AMP

You see, the whole world is filled with covetousness, lust and corruption. It is decaying.

For all that is in the world, the lust of the flesh, and the lust of the eyes, and the pride of life is not of the Father, but is of the world.

1 John 2:16

Believers can be caught up in that corruption: the lust, the greed, the power. They can be destroyed with the world — unless they are able to escape.

God did not intend for the Church to be destroyed along with the world. He planned an escape for us.

There is only one way to escape the world's corruption (lust of the flesh, lust of the eyes, pride of life and all the greed in our world today). That way of escape is through the *epignosis* — the exact, full, complete knowledge of God the Father and of Jesus Christ, His Son.

Our escape from that corruption is based upon our really knowing the Lord and being in the position to receive His promises.

Learn Your Background

As you learn more and more about your heavenly Father and His Son, Jesus Christ, you will better understand His promises. And the more you know God and understand His promises, the more you will be able to see yourself as you really are — in Him.

That's also true regarding your life here on earth. By understanding your father and mother — their characteristics, their habits, their beliefs — you are better able to understand yourself. The more you learn about what is inside them, the more you can understand about the things they put in you that determine how you act.

It's amazing how some people's lives have been changed as a result of their situation. They may have difficulty really knowing who they are because they don't really know and understand their family background.

A child can be abandoned by its real parents and adopted by another couple. Though brought up in love by the adoptive parents, the child will still have questions about the past. Often, as an adult, that person will then go looking for information about his or her real parents.

Such people are searching to find out who they really are. By learning the truth — whether good or bad — they get insight into their past, and that seems to shape their behavior. It's amazing how attitudes can be changed once people find out about their background and learn who they really are.

The same is true in the spiritual world. You need to learn about your heavenly Father, the spiritual Daddy from Whom you were born, and about His Son, Jesus Christ. The more you learn, the more insight you will receive regarding how you see yourself spiritually.

That *epignosis* will change the way you walk, the way you talk, the way you look at yourself. You will begin saying to yourself, *I have power to do whatever my heavenly Father said, because my Daddy is number one!* You will realize how all that your Father has is in you!

I have the attributes of my father and mother. I was raised by them, and they are in me. I look like them, act like them, think like them.

The same is true of *my* children. Sometimes I know just what my kids are thinking and what they are going to do, even before they do it. That's because when I look at them, I see myself. They seem always to be trying to pull the same maneuvers on me that I tried to pull on my mom and dad. My kids use the same tactics I did, because they have my genes in them!

So, being able to escape **the corruption that is in the world through lust** comes from having the knowledge of God — the *epignosis.*

Now if that is the only way you can escape being destroyed with the world, it would seem to me you would spend more time in the Word of God trying to get that knowledge.

Diligently Add to Your Faith

Let's go on to the next verse:

And beside this, giving all diligence, add to your faith.

2 Peter 1:5

This verse is saying, "Besides this — having already received His great and precious promises, being a partaker of His divine nature and escaping the corruption in the

15

world through lust — give all diligence and add to your faith."

Notice it says, **Add to your** *faith.*

The word *faith* in this verse does not mean your religious affiliation — whether Catholic, Baptist, Methodist, Episcopalian, or some other denomination. When born again, every believer has been given the measure of the God-kind of faith — the ability to believe His promises and appropriate them in this life.

There has been much teaching in the Body of Christ on the subject of faith. Sermons have been preached on how there is *great* faith, *little* faith, *strong* faith, *weak* faith.

You may know and understand this subject, but you need to realize that operating in faith alone is not enough. Understanding that you have the faith of God and knowing how to walk in strong faith is not enough.

Faith is important; it is the bedrock, the basis of our walk with God. God's Word says that without faith it is impossible to please God. (Heb. 11:6.)

But walking by faith alone is not enough. It takes more than just believing God for things. You can operate in faith and still stumble and fall. To be in a position to obtain the goal of never stumbling or falling, you need to add to your faith.

There are seven characteristics given in God's Word that must be added to your faith for you to be an individual who is not tricked by the enemy. Let's take a look at these characteristics.

2
Season Your Faith "Just Right"

There are seven ingredients which, when added to your faith, will cause you to never stumble and never fall. Let's look at these verses from Second Peter:

> And beside this, giving all diligence, add to your faith virtue; and to virtue knowledge;
>
> And to knowledge temperance; and to temperance patience; and to patience godliness;
>
> And to godliness brotherly kindness; and to brotherly kindness charity [or love].
>
> For if these things be in you, and abound, they make you that ye shall neither be barren nor unfruitful in the knowledge of our Lord Jesus Christ.
>
> But he that lacketh these things is blind, and cannot see afar off, and hath forgotten that he was purged from his old sins.
>
> Wherefore the rather, brethren, give diligence to make your calling and election sure: for if ye do these things, ye shall never [AMP: stumble or] fall.
>
> **2 Peter 1:5-10**

Let's read a portion of these verses from *The Amplified Bible:*

> ...adding your diligence [to the divine promises], employ every effort in *exercising* your faith to *develop* virtue (excellence, resolution, Christian energy); and in [exercising] virtue [develop] knowledge (intelligence),
>
> And in [exercising] knowledge [develop] self-control; and in [exercising] self-control [develop]

steadfastness (patience, endurance), and in [exercising] steadfastness [develop] godliness (piety),

And in [exercising] godliness [develop] brotherly affection, and in [exercising] brotherly affection [develop] Christian love.

2 Peter 1:5-7 AMP

By exercising our faith we can develop these seven characteristics: virtue, knowledge, self-control, steadfastness, godliness, brotherly affection and Christian love.

As we have read from the *King James Version*, verse 5 says:

> **And beside this, giving all diligence, *add to your faith*.**

These seven attributes must be added to the faith of God. Do you have the faith of God, or the God-kind of faith? That's what Jesus said we are to have. (Mark 11:22.)

Add Some Seasoning

Although you have been given that God-kind of faith, you have to add some seasoning to your faith. Faith just does not "taste right" until certain seasonings have been added to it.

Think of it like you would fried chicken. Now I happen to love fried chicken. But people season their chicken in different ways. The best-tasting fried chicken must have the proper amount of seasoning. After tasting some chicken, I just know some flavoring is missing. It needs a little help!

The same thing is true with our faith. There are seven seasonings that need to be added to make the "chicken of faith" taste right. Let's take a look at these attributes, one by one.

Virtue

Number 1: *Add to your faith virtue.*

I see virtue being like the hot sauce of faith. Chicken just does not taste right to me unless I can add some hot sauce to it! Some folks say I don't really know what chicken tastes like because I am always smothering it in hot sauce. But I don't want to know what chicken tastes like without that hot sauce!

The word *virtue* in the Greek means moral goodness, moral excellence.[1] In other words, it is saying you are to add morality to your faith.

You can believe God and have the faith to move mountains and speak the Word only; but if, at the same time, you are living an immoral life, you will stumble and fall, even with all your faith!

You can be a great giant of faith, who is able to believe God for healing, prosperity and all sorts of things. But you will still stumble and fall unless you are living a morally excellent life.

Do you know what morals are? I remember some words of Kenneth Hagin at Rhema Bible Training Center in Tulsa, Oklahoma. He said, "Some people have the morals of a back-alley cat."

People can sit in church and soak up the Word of God, then go out into the world and soak up something else.

If you are moral, you won't get AIDS. If you are living morally, you won't wind up in jail. If morality really means something to you, you will live accordingly.

Being moral means following the law.

What law? God's law.

---

[1] W. E. Vine, Merrill F. Unger and William White, Jr. *Vine's Complete Expository Dictionary of Old and New Testament Words.* (Nashville: Thomas Nelson, 1985), p. 661.

Sexual Immorality

God's law says a man and woman don't have sex unless they are married to each other. They have no business getting themselves into a predicament. According to today's world, this kind of thinking is just old-fashioned. But to me it's still right!

These days the word *love* is being used too freely. Guys are saying things to their girlfriends like: "I *really* love you, baby! And if you love me, you'll prove your love by giving yourself to me."

But real love always has commitment to it. If there is no commitment, then it's not really love; it's just lust. Remember, as we read in Second Peter 1:4, we have to escape the corruption that is in the world through lust.

There is so much corruption in the world today. Sexual diseases are running rampant, unwanted babies are being born every day, and millions of other babies have been aborted — killed! People are refusing to live in moral excellence, and because of that, we are seeing our whole nation stumbling and falling!

Stealing

By adding to your faith virtue, or moral excellence, you won't be stealing from others.

Today people are stealing from their own churches. They grab money out of the cash register in their church bookstore, or steal microphones and other equipment from their sanctuary. Then the next Sunday morning they sit in church and put on a front, looking so pious and religious.

All I would say to such a person is, "You're going to hell! You will stumble or fall, and you *will* be exposed! You had better give back what you have stolen, because it can cost you your life!"

Now if you want to keep from stumbling or falling, you need to be adding that moral excellence to your faith. You can be believing God, but you need to be living right, too.

You may say you want to believe God for financial blessings. If so, then make sure you are not stealing from your employer. You must be giving an honest day's work for an honest day's pay. If you have not worked honestly, then you should give back all that money you didn't work for!

You may be able to believe God for everything in the world, but unless you have moral excellence, you will fall flat on your face.

So, add that virtue, or moral excellence, to your faith, because your faith is not enough. You have to be living right! You can be believing God for things, yet still not be living your life as morally as you ought. God wants holiness from His people.

Morality — all boundaries of morality — is something our society has lost. These days anything and everything goes, no matter what it is. No one is supposed to question what is happening around them or say anything against it. We are not supposed to talk anymore about what is moral or immoral. Those of us with morality are told to shut our mouths, that somehow we are prudish and old-fashioned and dumb to believe in some form of basic morality.

Well, I'm not about to shut my mouth, and neither should you! It seems to me we have kept our mouths shut for too long while all kinds of filthiness have been going on around us.

So remember: as a believer, you need to add virtue, or morality, to your faith. (How's that for really putting on the hot sauce? I'm smothering that "chicken" with it!)

Knowledge

Number 2: *Add to virtue knowledge.*

As we learned earlier, the Greek word for "knowledge" in Second Peter 1:2,3 is *epignosis*. But in verse 5 the Greek word translated "knowledge" is *gnosis*[2].

Greek is a very expressive language. The same word as translated in English can have different meanings. Let's look at the word *love*, for instance.

In the English language when we say, "I love you," the word *love* covers everything. We could be saying, "I *love* cats, I *love* dogs, I *love* chicken and I *love* you." The one word *love* is used regarding all the different kinds of love.

But in the Greek language there are different words meaning "love." For instance, we could say, "I *agape* you[3]," meaning to love with the God-kind of love, or "I *phileo*[4] you," meaning to love as a friend.

The same is true with the word *knowledge.* In verse 5 it says:

> ...add to your faith virtue; and to virtue knowledge.

Now I like how *The Amplified Bible* renders verse 5. It says:

> **For this very reason, adding your diligence [to the divine promises], employ every effort in exercising your faith to develop virtue (excellence, resolution, Christian energy); and in [exercising] virtue [develop] knowledge (intelligence).**

The Greek word for knowledge, *gnosis*, means primarily a seeking to know, an inquiry, an investigation, particularly of spiritual truth.[5]

---

[2]Strong, "Greek Dictionary of the New Testament," p. 20, #1108.
[3]Ibid., p. 7, #26.
[4]Ibid., p. 75, #5368.
[5]W. E. Vine. *Expository Dictionary of New Testament Words.* (Old Tappan: Fleming H. Revell, 1940) Vol. II, p. 301, "gnosis."

You are to add to your faith inquiry and investigation, a seeking to know. Seeking *who*? Seeking God and His Word — questioning Him to find out His will and direction. Not only must you be an individual who can walk by faith and not by sight (2 Cor. 5:7), but you must always be inquiring to learn more about the things of God.

You should never take the position of saying, "I'm God's man [or woman] of faith and power, and I know it all!"

When you are hearing someone preach on a particular subject, you may think you already know enough about it. So instead of listening to what is being said, your mind goes off in some other direction. But you need to shut off your mind and open your spirit to receive from the Lord. Listen to the Holy Ghost and let Him teach you.

You should be seeking to know the will of God and then believing Him for what He wants you to do. In fact, it is much easier to exercise your faith when you have inquired of the Lord and have come to know His will. Then there will be no doubt whatsoever and you will have no problem believing God in that area. You will get results every time.

Verse 5 is saying, "Add *gnosis* — investigation, inquiry, intelligence." You are doing the intelligent thing by choosing to get into God's Word.

You should be seeking more knowledge from the Lord about a matter. God's Word says, **Seek ye the Lord, while he may be found, call ye upon him while he is near** (Isa. 55:6). Jesus tells us, **But seek ye first the kingdom of God, and his righteousness; and all these things shall be added unto you** (Matt. 6:33).

You are to add to your faith, but don't just be believing God for things.

You may ask God, "What should I be believing You for?" But before getting an answer, you decide what you will use your faith for. God has given you faith, but He wants you to ask Him how to use it and then wait for His direction.

You may be using your faith to believe Him for things you need, things you want. But just because you *want* something does not mean you *need* it. Find out first if it is something you should be believing God for. If you always got everything you wanted, your faith could be shipwrecked. Some people cannot handle certain things, and there are some things people just don't need.

Suppose somebody gave you a fifty-foot cabin cruiser. You might begin spending time out on your boat Sunday mornings, instead of sitting in church and hearing the Word of God. You don't need that distraction.

Instead of always using your faith to believe God for a new car, a new house or more money, you need to use your faith and believe God to be operating in the knowledge of God.

God wants you to use your faith to believe for things He wants done for other people.

When your faith is used to give to others and help meet their needs, the principle of God's Word applies. Then you can know it will be given back to you, good measure, pressed down, shaken together and running over. That's what Jesus said in Luke 6:38.

It's time for God's people to go to a higher level, to a higher calling.

It's time for us to walk in the vision God has given us to spread the Gospel to the world.

It's time for us to care that millions of people are going to hell without the saving knowledge of Jesus Christ.

It's time that we look beyond the circumference of our own houses and cars and fine clothes. There is nothing wrong with these things; God wants His people to be blessed — and we are His children — but He wants us to look past our own borders. We have to forget about our own program and start looking to His program.

Seeking more knowledge of God and His desires will help to accomplish His will in our lives.

Temperance

Number 3: *Add to knowledge temperance.*

In *The Amplified Bible* verse 6 says:

And in [exercising] knowledge [develop] self-control.

Notice the word *temperance* means *self*-control, not *God*-control.

People pray for God to control them, saying, "God, I want You to do this for me so I won't sin." But they don't need *God*-control; they need some *self*-control.

God is saying, "You use your faith to exercise self-control." You need to believe God in what He has put inside you.

Remember God's Word says, **...work out your own salvation with fear and trembling. For it is God which worketh in you both to will and to do of his good pleasure** (Phil. 2:12). God has put in you the ability, the power, the resolve to walk free from any sin, any lust of the flesh, any fear. But for it to come to pass, you must believe Him.

Exercise Self-Control

Now this is something we really need to do regarding a whole range of issues. For instance, we need to exercise self-control over our budget.

So often, people making $100 a week will spend $102 every week. If that includes you, then you are out of control! You need self-control. God cannot use you the way He wants to if you are bound up in debt. Start believing God to reign in your appetite for buying everything new that comes along!

God wants His people to be able to bless His Church so that His work can be done. He wants you giving money to the poor. When you do, He will give back to you — with interest! But you cannot do God's bidding if you have not exercised any self-control over your budget.

Or maybe you are not exercising self-control over your body. Maybe you are eating consistently — all day and all night! By letting your body get out of control where food is concerned, the power of God will not be able to work in you as it should!

This is why the Bible says: **What? know ye not that your body is the temple of the Holy Ghost which is in you, which ye have of God, and ye are not your own? For ye are bought with a price** (1 Cor. 6:19,20).

God is saying, "That's *My* body you are living in, and I want you to exercise some control over it."

Why does God care about that? Because there is a correlation between flowing in the Spirit and having self-control of the body.

When you learn to control your body, you can then use it to control everything else. So start exercising some self-control! God gave us a brain so we would use it.

Now in exercising self-control, there are some things we should not do. We should have enough sense not to put ourselves in the wrong position.

Why would extremely overweight people always be driving by a Dairy Queen on a hot summer day? They should be taking a different route.

Why would a single guy, who is supposed to be believing God, have to take cold showers to keep himself in line sexually? If that's his problem, he shouldn't be going to see R-rated movies. By putting himself in that position, he is just asking for trouble. Then he complains to his pastor that he can't control himself. He needs to begin exercising some *self*-control!

Why would a lady with a weakness for buying new dresses keep going into all those fancy and expensive dress shops? You might say, "I'm just looking because I like to shop." If that's really a problem, you had better get yourself out of there!

Peter was saying, "For you to keep from stumbling or falling, you must *add* some self-control to your faith and *exercise* that self-control!" In other words, "Use your brain!" God gave you a brain — not just so you would have something to slosh around inside your skull, but so you would have some brainpower to use. So start using it!

You won't stumble or fall when you can control yourself, your mouth and your actions. Peter would not have told you to add self-control to your faith unless you had the ability to do it. Yes, you *can* learn to control yourself. It can be done!

Patience

Number 4: *Add to temperance patience.*

Patience certainly is a virtue. It is learning how to wait on God.

In *The Amplified Bible*, verse 6 says:

...and in [exercising] self-control [develop] steadfastness (patience, endurance).

Patience means steadfastness, endurance, perseverance. Through patience you learn how to be steadfast, how to be unmoved, how to endure over a sustained period of time, how to persevere and keep on going, even through hard times.

These days we want everything in a hurry. We want it right now! After believing God for two months, we think that's long enough, that whatever we have been believing for should be manifested — now! But in the Word of God we can see how people believed God for years before certain things came to pass.

By adding to your faith some patience, endurance and steadfastness, you will learn how to *never* give up.

Godliness

Number 5: *Add to patience godliness.*

Godliness is holiness. This does not mean just living morally according to the world's standards and the basic standards of the Bible. It means living holy before God, walking in supernatural holiness. In other words, it is God-likeness, or being like God.

Did you know that you can walk in that supernatural holiness?

You should add to your faith these God-like qualities: act like God acts, talk like God talks and think the way God thinks, as He has taught us in His Word. This comes as our mind is being renewed.

In God's Word we are told to:

> ...present your bodies a living sacrifice, holy, acceptable unto God, which is your reasonable service. And be not conformed to this world: but *be ye transformed by the renewing* [Greek: renovation[6]] *of your mind,* that ye may prove what is that good, and acceptable, and perfect, will of God.
>
> **Romans 12:1,2**

6Ibid., p. 11, #342.

As you learn to think the way God thinks by spending time in His Word and beginning to think His way, you will strip off all the old ways you were taught to think.

Now you cannot add these God-like qualities to your faith if you do not spend enough time in His Word. You must have the full, exact knowledge of God to find out what all these God-like qualities are.

That's the intent of faith. God is saying, "I have given you this great faith. Now add the seasoning of godliness."

So, begin using your faith now to walk in holiness.

Brotherly Kindness

Number 6: *Add to godliness brotherly kindness.*

Verse 7, once again in *The Amplified Bible*, says it this way:

> **And in [exercising] godliness [develop] brotherly affection.**

You are to add brotherly affection or kindness to your faith. Make sure you find a way to do good to your brothers and sisters in Christ. Add affection for the saints: love them, help them, bless them.

Galatians 6:10 reads:

> **As we have therefore opportunity, let us do good unto all men, *especially* unto them who are of the household of faith.**

This is saying, "Do good to everybody, but take special care to help all those who are saved."

The Amplified Bible renders it this way:

> **So then, as occasion and opportunity open to us, let us do good (morally) to all people [not only being useful or profitable to them, but also doing what is for their spiritual good and advantage]. Be mindful to be a**

blessing, especially to those of the household of faith — those who belong to God's family with you, the believers.

God cares about all people. But His Word says those who are saved should be more of a family to you than those who happen to share your bloodline and the same last name.

God is saying, "Especially do good to other Christians." When God looks at "the family," He is not looking at the bloodline based on the way we look at it. He sees "the family" as those who are in Christ.

If we are supposed to operate by faith and in the Word of God, how could one Christian take advantage of another? How could one overcharge another? How could one commit to do a job for another and then not finish that work? How could any Christians do wrong to their brothers and sisters in Christ?

Our brothers and sisters in Christ are our *real* family.

Thank God for relatives. Most of my relatives are born again (and I praise God for that!), but I am believing God for the rest of them. Maybe you too have some relatives that are not saved. Did you know God expects us to do better to fellow Christians than to our unsaved relatives?

From God's perspective, if we do wrong to another Christian, we are doing wrong to Him! He takes a personal affront whenever we do wrong to another born-again believer. He said, **Let us do good...especially unto them who are of the household of faith.**

So be sure you are doing good to your brothers and sisters in the Lord. When you say to another believer, "I love you in Jesus' name," you should not just *say* it; you should *do* it by showing love to that believer.

We are to be the most considerate toward other believers.

Let's say a handicapped person or senior citizen comes in late to a church service. That person should not have to hunt for a place to sit. So what if he or she should have been there earlier? It is still our responsibility to do good to that person. An outside seat on a row toward the front of the sanctuary should be offered quickly. We should want to do good to the household of faith.

Suppose so many people are attending a service that all the seats are taken and some are standing, as happens sometimes in our church. Men ought to value their born-again sisters enough to offer them their seats. So what if a lady comes in late when she should have been on time? Some gentleman should get up immediately and offer his seat!

I believe, too, that it is good for boys, while they are still boys, to learn how to act toward ladies. Then they will already know it when they are grown. My son knows to open doors for the ladies. Not because the ladies could not do it themselves. I know they are liberated. I know they are strong. This has nothing to do with them being liberated or strong; it has to do with the fact that they are our sisters in the Lord and we want to honor them!

I remember the first time I took my wife out on a date. When I drove her home and stopped in front of her house, she immediately opened the car door to get out. I said, "Don't you open that door!" Then I got out, walked around to her side and opened it for her.

Deborah looked at me in shock. She had never in her life seen a man act like that. She couldn't believe I was for real. But she liked what she saw!

So God's Word is saying, "Add brotherly kindness to your faith, especially being sure that you take care of those in the household of faith."

Charity, or Love

There is one more addition to our faith:

Number 7: *Add to brotherly kindness charity.*

...and in [exercising] brotherly affection [develop] Christian love.

2 Peter 1:7 AMP

This charity, or Christian love, is the God-kind of love. The Greek word here is *agape*[7], the God-quality of love, the kind of love God functions in. That love is unselfish love, the kind of love that always operates in forgiveness. You find it described in First Corinthians, chapter 13.

The God-kind of love is not dependent on feelings, saying, "I will love you if you treat me good." Instead it says, "I will love you regardless of what you do." That's the way God is. If He didn't love us like that, we would be in big trouble!

We all have messed up somewhere in our lives. We have committed spiritual adultery against God, seeking first after other things instead of Him. But He continued loving us, regardless of what we had done.

God is saying, "To be like Me, you must add that kind of love to your faith."

What is God? He is love. He is peace. He is joy. He is holy. These are God-like qualities that should be added to our faith.

Some people know how to confess God's Word. By learning Scriptures like Mark 11:23, they know how to speak against mountains and see them removed. But they will stumble and fall if there is no real love — God's love — functioning in their lives. The Word of God tells us that faith works, or operates, by love. (Gal. 5:6.)

Love is the ultimate God-like quality.

You add this God-like quality of love to your faith, and you will begin believing God for others instead of yourself.

---

[7]Ibid., p. 7, #26.

You will be believing God to save the lost instead of spending all your time praying for God to take care of your own needs. You will care about people being saved. You will care about the work of the Lord being done, because the work of the Lord is to help others.

You will care not just in your heart but in your actions. You will believe God for food to give to the homeless, for clothes to give to the naked. You will believe Him to help you have time to visit the sick. You will believe Him for money to give into His work so that others may be saved. You will care about what's happening in all the cities of America, and you will want to see His ministry spread throughout the globe!

These Things Should Abound in You

After listing these seven ingredients to be added to our faith, the apostle Peter said:

For if these things be in you, and abound... (v. 8).

The word *if* is important in this verse. You see, this is not just automatic. Peter had said in verse 5, **Add to your faith.** The understood subject of that sentence is *you.* He was saying, "*You* add it. *You* make sure this happens. *You* concentrate on this."

Then he says, *If* **these things be in you, and abound....** These things should be growing and developing in you.

For if these things be in you, and abound, they make you that ye shall neither be barren nor unfruitful in the knowledge of our Lord Jesus Christ.
2 Peter 1:8

Here is an important point in this verse: that we **neither be barren nor unfruitful in the knowledge of our Lord Jesus Christ.**

Then Peter goes on in verse 9 to say:

But he that lacketh these things is blind, and cannot see afar off, and hath forgotten that he was purged from his old sins.

The Amplified Bible says it this way:

For whoever lacks these qualities is blind, [spiritually] shortsighted, seeing only what is near to him [In other words, he can't see the forest for the trees!]; and has become oblivious [of the fact] that he was cleansed from his old sins.

If you don't add these qualities to your faith, you won't be able to keep from sinning. But when you add them to your faith, you will *never* stumble and *never* fall.

3

Having a Vital Knowledge of God

Let's look again at a portion of Scripture from Second Peter:

> **Grace and peace be multiplied unto you.**
>
> **2 Peter 1:2**

Grace and peace be *what*? Be *multiplied*!

Multiplication is much better than addition. We know that 2 plus 2 is 4, and 4 plus 4 is 8. But in multiplication, 4 *times* 4 is 16. We can double and triple quickly when we start to multiply!

In this verse you can read how God's grace and peace are being **multiplied unto you**; but unless you really know God, you will not know about His grace and peace.

Let's look at this verse from *The Amplified Bible*. It gives six definitions for the word *peace*. See if you have need of these six things:

> **May grace (God's favor) and peace, (which is *perfect well-being, all necessary good, all spiritual prosperity* and *freedom from fears and agitating passions and moral conflicts*) be multiplied to you.**
>
> **2 Peter 1:2 AMP**

Again, the six definitions of peace listed here are:

#1 perfect well-being

#2 all necessary good

#3 all spiritual prosperity

#4   freedom from fears

#5   freedom from agitating passions

#6   freedom from moral conflict

Let's consider some of these definitions of peace.

Freedom From Fear

As was mentioned previously in this study, God's peace gives you freedom from *all* fears.

This would be of great concern to people full of fear. Fear seems to consume so many areas of their lives. They live with fear of failure, fear of getting hurt, fear of being rejected, fear of hunger, fear that their children won't succeed, fear that they are not smart enough, fear of being left alone all the days of their lives. (There may be other kinds of fear that come to your mind.)

The apostle Peter was saying to the Church, "May God's peace and freedom from that fear be multiplied to you through the *epignosis* — the exact, full knowledge of God and of Jesus our Lord."

Now remember what we read in verse 8:

If these things be in you, and abound, they make you that ye shall neither be barren nor unfruitful in the knowledge of our Lord Jesus Christ.

With the words **these things** here in verse 8, Peter was referring to the seven characteristics he had listed previously in verses 5-7. When **these things** are added to your faith — when they are **in you, and abound** — you will bring forth fruit as you come to know more and more about the Lord Jesus Christ.

If you have been fearful, you can now experience the freedom from those fears. It is available to you because, as verse 8 says, it has been **multiplied unto you through the**

knowledge of God. This aspect of God's peace will help to keep you from never stumbling or falling.

Perfect Well-being

How about **perfect well-being** as a definition of peace? Think of this also being **multiplied unto you**.

With perfect well-being, you can really be in peace, no matter what may be going on around you. The economy can be bad. People can be killing people. Some crazy things can be going on in your neighborhood. But regardless of all the bad things happening around you, by living in Jesus you can keep a smile on your face. Now that's having perfect well-being!

With this perfect well-being you can be at peace with yourself. That peace is multiplied to you through the knowledge of God the Father and of Jesus our Lord.

Freedom From Agitating Passions

This aspect of peace makes you able to control your temper.

Temper makes the blood pressure go up. It gets people into trouble, making them say things they should never have said and do things they should never have done. Later they wonder, *Why in the world did I do and say those things?* But they were angry because of those agitating passions.

There are a variety of agitating passions, and maybe you can think of some other area. But regardless of the kind you have had to deal with, you can have the peace of God. It has been multiplied unto you through the exact, full knowledge of the Father and of His Son, Jesus Christ.

These Things Should *Abound* in You

I want us to take another look at Second Peter 1:8, which says:

For *if* these things be in you....

The word *if* here tells us it is possible for these things not to be functioning in us.

These things will not automatically develop and manifest in you. There is a decision you must make.

It is not enough that you have only a portion of these things. You cannot just walk a little bit in love, a little bit in self-control and kindness, a little bit in holiness and moral excellence. Verse 8 says:

For if these things be in you, *and abound*....

If these things are abounding in you, it means they are growing by leaps and bounds.

For if these things be in you, and abound, they make you that ye shall neither be barren nor unfruitful in the knowledge of our Lord Jesus Christ.

2 Peter 1:8

Peter could have said, "If these things be in you and abound, then you will be blessed from head to toe." But that's not what he said! He was saying, "If all these things are abounding in you, you shall not be barren or unfruitful in the knowledge of Jesus."

The big prize is having the knowledge of the Lord Jesus Christ.

After you have added all seven of those ingredients to your faith, you will reach the place where they abound. Then you will have that knowledge — *epignosis* — the exact, full knowledge of the Lord Jesus Christ. That's the key thing. Remember what we read in verse 2:

Grace and peace be multiplied unto you *through the knowledge* of God, and of Jesus our Lord.

Having *real* knowledge — either of God or of another person — is vital.

How You Learn About Someone

If you want to really learn about another person, there are four areas you should know about that person.

As an example, let's consider a single person who is thinking seriously about marriage. Maybe this fits your situation right now. If so, learning these four areas about the person you want to marry would help you to make sure that is the right person for you.

Knowing the History

First of all, you would want to find out the history of that person. You especially would want to know the health history, considering the problems people face these days. You also would want to know the financial history.

Having done some post-marital counseling, I have heard some interesting stories. In one situation, the wife found out her husband had been through three bankruptcies and was still $100,000 in debt. The only problem was, he did not tell her about it until *after* they were married! That man is the product of what has happened in his life.

At least by understanding an individual's history, you can better understand the person.

Knowing That Person's Culture

Secondly, you need to have an understanding of that person's culture — where he [or she] was raised and the kind of people he grew up around. Culture matters. It matters at least in being able to understand the individual you are thinking seriously about marrying. Cultural differences can collide if you don't understand why.

For instance, the cultures between a small family and a large family are quite different. My wife and I have known personally a real cultural difference in this way.

Deborah comes from a large family; she has nine brothers and three sisters. Now that's large! Big families like that must have lots of fun. Besides, nobody would ever mess with her, knowing she had nine brothers to take her side!

On the other hand, I was raised in a small family. I am the oldest of three.

My mama was a housewife until I was fourteen or fifteen years old. Every evening she served a complete dinner. I remember how when our dad came home from work, the table was already set. When we heard him drive up, we ran to the table and waited until he took his place there. Then Mama served the meal. I was really blessed to be raised in that kind of culture. Today families just don't live like that, but that's how it was with us.

With this in mind, you can see how Deborah and I were raised differently.

When we first got married, I saw things based on my cultural background, so I expected dinner to be the way my mama did it. When I came home from work and turned in the driveway, I expected there to be a formal place setting at the table like I had been accustomed to. In my mind, that's just the way it was supposed to be.

But Deborah, having come from a large family with thirteen kids sitting around the table, was not used to all that.

I remember the first time I went into her family's kitchen. I had never seen a commercial kettle before. It was huge! And there it was — full of spaghetti! I couldn't believe what I saw next. Everybody ran in, picked up a paper plate, filled it with spaghetti and sat down to eat. And if you didn't get there in time to eat, too bad!

We came from two different cultures. One was not superior to the other. They were just two different ways of doing things. Only I didn't really realize the cultural differences. But I learned some things after we were married!

I will never forget the first day I came home from work. I was looking forward to the kind of meal my mama always served. I expected china to be set on the table. After all, my wife wasn't working, so I thought everything would be waiting on me. What did I find? A paper plate, a styrofoam cup, some spaghetti and some Koolaid.

I hit the roof. "What is this?" I said.

I felt my wife was being disrespectful of me as a man, but I didn't know what I had done to deserve that disrespect. And I wanted to know why I was having to eat off a paper plate. I just never ate off paper plates — never! So I threw a fit.

I know Deborah wondered what I was creating all that fuss about. She didn't know why I was so upset and she thought I was being ridiculous. So she got mad at me. We ended up having a little tit for tat.

All that happened because we really did not understand each other's culture. Once we both realized some things about culture, we were able to work together.

Now you must understand that you can be born again, filled with the Holy Ghost, and still have a tit for tat with your new spouse. Eventually, real life is going to set in. So you need to understand culture.

Learning To Really Communicate

The third point you need to consider about that person is whether he [or she] has the ability to really share some innermost feelings and thoughts. You need to talk and communicate over an extended period of time.

It's more than just talking nice to that person, saying things like, "Honey, you're so fine, so special."

Real communication is absolutely necessary.

Observing That Person's Actions

To really know someone, there is a fourth thing you have to do: observe his [or her] actions over an extended period of time.

This way you will be able to see if what he *does* corresponds with what he *says*.

Getting To Know God

Much of this is true about knowing God. As we read in verse 2:

> **Grace and peace be multiplied unto you** *through the knowledge* **of God.**

Remember this verse says, **Grace and peace...**, and remember too that, as we read from *The Amplified Bible*, God's peace has six meanings. All this happens through the knowledge of God the Father. This is one reason you need to study the Old Testament as well as the New Testament. This grace and peace are to be multiplied unto you through the exact, full knowledge of God.

So, how do you get to know God?

By Learning God's History

One of the ways you get to know God is by studying and learning His past. Again, you need to study both the Old and the New Testaments.

Much of God's history is found in the Old Testament. By reading the Old Testament books, you will see how God interacted with His people in those days. You will see how He dealt with them in Genesis and Exodus, in Numbers and Deuteronomy, in Joshua and Judges and Ruth, in First and Second Samuel, and on and on.

By Learning God's Culture

By reading God's history, you will also come to know about God's culture. You will understand how He really acts and why some things are the way they are today.

We know what God's culture is: He is holy — period!

By Communicating With God

Another way to get to know God is by spending time in communication with Him. He communicates to you through His Word, then you communicate with Him. By communicating with the Lord over an extended period of time, you will come to know Him. You can observe His actions and know how He works through time.

People are always asking, "How do you know the voice of God?"

Just the way you get to know the voice of anybody else. If you hang around that person long enough, you will learn his voice. It's the same with God.

I don't have to see my wife to know when she is in the room. I can just hear that voice speaking to another person, and I know it's Deborah. We have been together for twenty years, so I know her voice well.

In the same way, I have learned about the flow of the Holy Ghost by seeing how He has moved over the years. There are certain things I can just see happening. I don't have to hear the Lord speaking to me; I just know what is coming next because I know how He moves at times.

Knowing God Through Jesus

Now notice again verse 2. It says:

> **Grace and peace be multiplied unto you through the knowledge of God, and of Jesus our Lord.**
> **2 Peter 1:2**

> May grace (God's favor) and peace...be multiplied
> to you in (the full, personal, precise and correct)
> knowledge of God and of Jesus our Lord.
>
> **2 Peter 1:2** AMP

The reason God gave us the New Testament was so that
we could come to understand Jesus, the Son of God.
Remember Jesus said, **He that hath seen me hath seen the
Father** (John 14:9). This is why we are to spend time in
God's Word. Grace and peace being multiplied to us is
dependent upon that. Coming to a place where we never
stumble or fall is dependent upon that.

This Scripture verse does not say that grace and peace
will be multiplied to you just *through knowledge.* There is
more involved than just getting information. There is some
particular information you must obtain. It says, **Grace and
peace be multiplied unto you through the** *knowledge of
God, and of Jesus our Lord.*

Through Him We Are Given All Things

> According as his divine power hath given unto us
> all things that pertain unto life and godliness, through
> the knowledge of him that hath called us to glory and
> virtue.
>
> **2 Peter 1:3**

This verse tells us, **His divine power has bestowed
upon us all things that are [requisite and suited] to life**
(AMP).

This happened when God raised Jesus from the dead.
That's when these things were provided for us through
Jesus.

Notice this verse says: **According as his divine power
hath given unto us** *all* **things.**

What does the word *all* mean? It means *everything*!

How much is left after *all*? Nothing!

...his divine power hath given unto us all things that pertain unto life and godliness, through — the *epignosis* — the knowledge of him that hath called us to glory and virtue.

We are able to receive all those things He has given us through Jesus being raised from the dead. All the promises of God are appropriated through the exact knowledge of God — knowing Who He is, knowing His character and nature.

We Are Partakers of His Divine Nature

Whereby are given unto us exceeding great and precious promises: that by these ye might be partakers of the divine nature, having escaped the corruption that is in the world through lust.

2 Peter 1:4

Let's read it from *The Amplified Bible*:

By means of these He has bestowed on us His precious and exceedingly great promises, so that through them you may escape (by flight) from the moral decay (rottenness and corruption) that is in the world because of covetousness (lust and greed), and become sharers (partakers) of the divine nature.

The more you become a partaker of the nature of God, the more you will act like God and the less you will stumble or fall. You see, God does not make errors. There is no stumbling or falling with Him.

World's Standards vs. God's Standard

God is saying you need to appropriate His precious and exceedingly great promises so that you will escape the world's lust, greed and corruption.

In the world's system we are taught the world's lust, the world's greed, the world's covetousness. As a result, we get caught up in a system which eventually causes us to fall down and hurt ourselves.

When you start thinking and acting like the world, you begin trying to accumulate all the things the world accumulates. Then you start measuring whether you are a success by the world's standards instead of God's standard.

You see, God's standard is not based on success in this world — whether you have three cars, or live in a mansion in the suburbs, or have a college degree, or see your name printed often in the newspaper. With God, none of these things equals success.

When you get wrapped up in the world's system and the world's covetousness, then instead of acting upon God's promises to you, you begin to think the world's way. What happens when you do that? You start putting pressure on yourself to obtain the things of this world.

Let me give you a real-life example. As a pastor I have seen this occur many times, in both males and females. I will use an example from the female side of life.

Many times over the years when counselling married couples, I have found that the woman has lost respect for the man. Because of that, she no longer sees him the same as when they were first married. At the beginning, he was her prince and he could do no wrong. When he came home to her, she never had rollers in her hair. She always wanted to look good for him.

But somewhere along the way, she lost respect for him. I have seen myriads of cases like this. That's why I use it as an example.

She becomes angry with him because he has not met the standard she expected, based upon the things she has seen accomplished by her girlfriends' husbands.

Her husband might be a professional man, maybe even a schoolteacher. Though schoolteachers are not poverty-stricken, they certainly do not make $100,000 a year. Maybe he has his bachelor's degree and has done all the things necessary to have that teaching job. He probably makes $25,000-$30,000 a year. But her girlfriends' husbands are managers or in some other fields. They might not have as much education as her husband, but they make more money.

So what happens? She looks at their homes. She compares their cars. She hears how they went away to some fancy place on their vacation. Her husband only gets time off for three days, while her friends can go away for a whole month. She compares things by looking at them in the world's way.

I have counselled situations like this many a day, and I see what has happened. The husband is doing all he can. In fact, he has done the right thing by going to school and bettering himself. He is a professional, but in his profession he can only go so far. There is a cap, a ceiling, a limit on the salary he can receive in that job.

So he is under pressure to give up his profession. The reason he went into it was because he loved it. But he may have to give up his profession in order for his wife to care for him again. And that's wrong!

This is a real-life example of what the Bible is talking about in Second Peter 1:4. When we have placed in ourselves the attributes of God, we will not view our spouse that way, whether husband or wife.

These days guys want women to make as much as they make, or more. At one time, only the woman decided if she would marry a man based on his income. Now the man decides to marry based on the woman's income.

When people have the wrong idea, stress comes against the marriage. Problems develop, causing a breakup, and divorce comes as a result. Why? Because those people have been corrupted in the world's idea of lust and covetousness. They have to keep up with the Joneses.

But that's not what God teaches His people.

God does not teach us to view our spouse and success based upon any such criteria. If we do, we will only stumble and fall, and we will be destroyed because of it.

Sometimes in those situations, husbands or wives see another person who is more successful than their spouse. After a while, they become friends with that person and say, "I sure wish my husband [or wife] was like you." Right then they become open to temptation in that area. Eventually, they will stumble or fall in their Christian walk. Why? Because they were caught by the world's corruption through lust.

As we read from *The Amplified Bible*: **By means of...His precious and exceedingly great promises...you may escape...the moral decay...lust and greed, and become sharers (partakers) of the divine nature** (2 Peter 1:4).

We are to take on those **precious and exceedingly great promises,** learning more about the nature of our heavenly Father and of His Son, the Lord Jesus Christ. We then add to our faith the seven virtues given in verses 5-7, until **these things be in you, and abound** (v. 8).

We will then be able to see our spouse the way we should — through the love of God. We will appreciate our spouse and be grateful for what he or she is doing. That's what God teaches us. As a result, we will not end up somewhere down the road in lust and greed. We will stay steady on our feet and will neither stumble nor fall.

Decide To Be Diligent

Now notice verses 4 and 5:

Whereby are given unto us exceeding great and precious promises: that by these ye might be partakers of the divine nature, having escaped the corruption that is in the world through lust.

And beside this, giving all diligence....

Here is another key to operating from the standpoint of never stumbling or falling. This requires a decision.

You must be an individual who decides to "give all diligence." You need to add diligence. Diligence is merely a decision, and then the execution of that decision.

Deciding to be diligent about something starts with small things. For instance, being in church on time is just a decision about being diligent.

You may say, "But I have lots to do to get my kids there on time."

Then you need to get up earlier. If that's too early, then go to the later service.

This Scripture is saying: "Add diligence to your study of God the Father. Add diligence to your study of His Son, the Lord Jesus Christ. Add diligence to the Promises, and when you do, you will develop to a place where you will never stumble or fall."

That is the goal: to be in a position where you neither stumble nor fall.

As we have read in verse 10, it tells us to **give diligence to make your calling and election sure: for if ye do these things, ye shall never** [AMP: stumble or] **fall.**

Then verse 11 says:

> **For so an entrance shall be ministered unto you abundantly into the everlasting kingdom of our Lord and Saviour Jesus Christ.**

This is the ultimate goal: that you receive the entrance already provided for you into the kingdom of our Lord Jesus Christ.

That entrance has been provided. You simply must be an individual who is diligent to do the things I am sharing in this book.

Get this truth into your spirit and understand what I am saying. Decide to be diligent. It can change your life as you learn more about how to never stumble or fall. Hallelujah!

4
The Rock of
Revelation Knowledge

I want to give you two scriptural examples of the value that comes from having the *true* knowledge from God. You will see, first of all, how someone received from God the exact knowledge of Jesus, then how that same person forgot the knowledge God had given him.

Who Jesus Is

Let's look first in Matthew, chapter 16. We will begin reading with verse 15:

> When Jesus came into the coasts of Caesarea Philippi, he asked his disciples, saying, Whom do men say that I the Son of man am?
>
> And they said, Some say that thou art John the Baptist: some, Elias; and others, Jeremias, or one of the prophets.
>
> He saith unto them, But whom say ye that I am?

Jesus was asking His disciples, "What are people saying about Me? Who do they say I am?"

The disciples gave Him various answers, but He asked them specifically, "Then who do *you* say I am?"

The answer was spoken by Peter, but it came straight from Almighty God!

> And Simon Peter answered and said, Thou art the Christ, the Son of the living God.

51

> **And Jesus answered and said unto him, Blessed art thou, Simon Barjona:** *for flesh and blood hath not revealed it unto thee, but my Father which is in heaven.*
> **Matthew 16:16,17**

I want you to notice the word *revealed* in this last verse.

Jesus was saying to Peter: "You didn't get this because somebody told it to you. You don't really realize Who I am because you heard it somewhere. Flesh and blood did not reveal it to you; it was given to you from My Father in heaven." In other words, Jesus was saying, "Peter, God the Father revealed to you Who I really am."

There are many people, even in churches, who *know* something about Jesus. They have heard His name mentioned time and time again. But they have yet to receive the revelation of Who Jesus really is. Colossians 1:27 says, **Christ in you, the hope of glory.**

I have been told who my parents are: Robert Butler is my father and Ida LaJean Butler is my mother. I can believe they are because I look and act just like them, but I don't really *know* that for sure.

Neither do you know about your parents. You were told that they are your mama and daddy. But you don't really know. You just hope that's the truth.

But knowing Jesus — knowing Who He really is — must be *revealed* to your spirit man. You cannot just *hope* it is true; you must believe it and receive that revelation knowledge in your heart.

The Rock of Revelation Knowledge

Jesus said to Peter:

> ...for flesh and blood hath not revealed it unto thee, but my Father which is in heaven.
> And I say also unto thee, That thou art Peter....
> **Matthew 16:17,18**

Now the word *Peter* in the Greek is *Petros*, which means rock[1]. Jesus was saying to him, "Peter, you're a big rock."

Then He said:

> ...and upon this *rock* I will build my church.
> **Matthew 16:18**

In the Greek the word translated "rock" is not *Petros*, but *petra*, which means a huge rock[2], like the Rock of Gibraltar.

Jesus said, "Peter, you are a big rock, and **upon this rock,** I will build My Church." The "rock" Jesus referred to was the revelation of Who He was. God the Father had given Peter this revelation. That's when he said to Jesus, **Thou art the Christ, the Son of the living God** (v. 16). Then Jesus said, **...upon *this rock* I will build my church** (v. 18).

Peter knew Jesus by name. He had walked and talked with Him. He had seen the miracles Jesus had performed. But even though Peter had been with Jesus, God had to reveal to him Who Jesus really was.

Jesus was saying, "Upon this rock of the Father revealing the Son, I will build My Church." The Church of the Lord Jesus Christ is the result of receiving that revealed knowledge of Him.

Supernatural Revelation of Jesus

Remember what we have read in Second Peter:

> **Grace and peace be multiplied unto you through the knowledge of God, and of Jesus our Lord.**
> **2 Peter 1:2**

---

[1]Strong, "Greek Dictionary of the New Testament," p. 57, #4074.

[2]Ibid., #4073. See also W. E. Vine, *Expository Dictionary of New Testament Words* (Old Tappan: Fleming H. Revell, 1940) Vol. III, p. 302, "rock."

As we have discussed previously, Peter then lists the characteristics each believer should add to his faith: virtue [or moral excellence], knowledge, self-control, patience [or steadfastness], godliness, brotherly kindness and Christian love.

In verse 8 Peter said:

> **For if *these things* be in you, and abound, they make you that ye shall neither be barren nor unfruitful in the knowledge of our Lord Jesus Christ.**

Then in verse 10 he said:

> **...if ye do *these things* ye shall never** [AMP: stumble or] **fall.**

The real key to never stumbling or falling is having the supernatural revelation of Who Jesus is.

You can go to church regularly and hear lots of preaching about Jesus. You can even read about Him in the Bible. But you have to genuinely understand the truth of Who Jesus is.

Once you have received that true revelation of Jesus and know Who is in you by the power of the Holy Ghost, you will be able to do those things Peter listed in his epistle. Then, according to the Scriptures, you will *never* stumble or fall!

That is supernatural revelation!

The Gates of Hell Shall Not Prevail!

Jesus said:

> **...upon this rock I will build my church; and the gates of hell shall not prevail against it.**
>
> **Matthew 16:18**

The gates of hell cannot withstand the Church that has received the supernatural revelation of Jesus. The gates of hell cannot stop God's people. Not only will we not stumble

54

or fall, but as His army we will go and take from Satan everything he has and every person he has controlled!

When the Word of God says the gates of hell shall not prevail against the Church, God's view is not that the gates of hell are surrounding the Church and the Church is being bombarded. The Church is not on the defense. That's not the role God sees of His Church.

God sees the Church as an army that is *already* free, *already* delivered. God's army is not stumbling or falling. His army is anointed by the Holy Ghost. That means we are filled with the power of God and the Greater One dwells on the inside of us. (1 John 4:4.)

As we see Who Jesus is, we can become like the apostle Paul, who said, **That I may know him, and the power of his resurrection** (Phil. 3:10). Paul wanted to know Jesus as He really was, seeing Him in His glorious power — when He threw off the principalities and powers, and made an open show of Satan. (Col. 2:15.)

God sees the gates of hell surrounding those who are not saved that keeps them in the compound of sin. But He sees the Church of the Lord Jesus Christ kicking open those gates and tearing down those walls. He sees the Church snatching away from Satan the sick and the lost and the hurting, then bringing them into the kingdom of God.

Really Seeing Jesus!

The gates of hell shall not prevail against the Church because they have seen Jesus; they have seen His glory.

That's like what happened to Paul when he said he was taken into the third heaven and heard things that were not lawful to utter. He saw things he could not describe. (2 Cor. 12:1-4.) He saw the glory of Jesus! Paul was so filled with His glory that even when faced with beatings and stonings and shipwrecks, he could not be killed. When a poisonous viper came out of the fire and bit him, it had no power over him. He had seen the glory of God! (2 Cor. 11:25; Acts 28:3-6.)

That was like the apostle John who told in the book of Revelation how he had seen Jesus on the isle of Patmos. When John saw Jesus, he described how His eyes were like a flame of fire. (Rev. 1:14.) He really saw Jesus!

I want you to know this: when you have seen Jesus in the fullest, you will *never* be the same. After that, the gates of hell will *never* prevail against you!

One of the reasons bad things can happen to members of the Church is because they have not really seen Jesus; they don't really know who they are in Him. But once they find out who they are and see Him as He really is, they won't easily give in to sin anymore. They won't be defeated anymore. They won't just sit in the church house; they will go out into the highways and hedges and compel the lost to come in. (Luke 14:23.)

When you have seen Jesus in this way — when you have received the exact and full knowledge of God — you will want everyone to have what you have.

As God's people, we need to get away from just having a form of godliness and denying the power thereof. (2 Tim. 3:5.)

Jesus said:

> **...upon this rock I will build my church; and the gates of hell shall not prevail against it.**
>
> **And I will give unto thee the keys of the kingdom of heaven: and whatsoever thou shalt bind on earth shall be bound in heaven.**
>
> **Matthew 16:18,19**

Whatever you declare bound shall be bound and whatever you loose shall be loosed — once it has been supernaturally revealed to you Who Jesus is.

But you can only get that way when you add all those ingredients to your faith; when you are walking in the love and holiness of God, operating in the peace of God, loving your brethren, exercising self-control. You will always be inquiring about God, seeking to know even more about Him.

There is more to Jesus than just what you read on the pages of your Bible. If you think you will really know Jesus only by reading those pages, you are wrong. You have to meditate on the truths of that Book and live according to the verses we have read in Second Peter. Then you will understand more of Jesus.

Maybe you have been married to the same person for many years, but you still don't know everything there is to know about that person. Deborah and I have been married for nineteen years, but from time to time I find something new in her. And I thought I knew her! There is always more to a person than you know. Some people have been married their entire lives and still never know all about each other.

The same thing is true regarding your Christian walk. No matter how many years you may have known Jesus as your Lord and Savior, you still don't know everything about Him, and you don't know everything about the power of God.

According to Matthew 16:19, which we just read, Jesus has given you the keys of the Kingdom, but those keys are wrapped in revelation knowledge.

Then the Storm Comes, Bringing Fear

Now I want to show you something else about this same Peter. After walking and talking with the Lord, he had received the first revelation of Who Jesus really was. Let me show you what happened to him and how there was more for him to learn.

In Mark, chapter 4, Jesus ministered the parable of the sower, followed by several other parables. He shared with that multitude of people how the power of God works and how the Word of God can produce a hundredfold in their lives. When He had finished ministering the entire message, He sent the people away.

> **And the same day, when the even was come, he saith unto them, Let us pass over unto the other side.**
>
> **And when they had sent away the multitude, they took him even as he was in the ship. And there were also with him other little ships.**
>
> **And there arose a great storm of wind, and the waves beat into the ship, so that it was now full.**
>
> **Mark 4:35-37**

When the wind blows with a gale-like force, waves can beat against a ship. The more the wind blows, the higher the waves will come, slapping against the boat. There was so much water coming against the disciples' boat that it was filled up.

Can you imagine being in a storm so horrific? So much water was pouring into their boat that it was rocking and reeling in that storm.

> **And he [Jesus] was in the hinder part of the ship, asleep on the pillow.**
>
> **Mark 4:38**

Sometimes we can read the Bible in such a religious way, but I want you to shut off your religious thinking and see this the way it could easily have happened.

Let's say they are out in the middle of some huge lake, like Lake Michigan, for instance. They are in a boat the size of a fifty-foot cabin cruiser. Only it isn't a cruiser, and it has no cabins.

Then a huge gale comes up. With water splashing against the boat, it is quickly being filled.

Things get so bad that the people on board become consumed with fear. They begin to sob, wondering if they are about to die.

Though a great storm was raging, Jesus was asleep in the back of the boat, with His head resting on a pillow.

That's the way things happen in our lives. There are times when a great storm arises. Situations occur. Someone dies. The family splits up. Financial crisis comes. Cancer or some other ungodly thing comes our way. Crises happen in our lives.

Wave after wave, that great storm keeps coming, snapping and slapping against you. First, one wave hits; then another wave hits; then another, and another, until finally your "boat" is full.

Then you begin to question God: "God, what's the matter? What's going on? What's the problem?"

When those waves hit against the disciples' boat where Jesus was asleep on that pillow, what did they do? They went straight to Jesus:

> ...and they awake him, and say unto him, Master, carest thou not that we perish?
>
> **Mark 4:38**

They were saying, "Master, wake up! We're about to die! Don't You care?"

They did not really know Who He was.

Just that day He had preached a sermon, teaching them how to cause the Word of God to produce one hundredfold. He had told them in a parable how Satan would come against them to immediately take away the Word that was sown. Then He issued a little bit of the Word of God to them when He said, **Let us pass over unto the other side** (v. 35). Satan came immediately to steal the Word that had been sown.

Though Jesus was lying in the back of that ship, the disciples had decided, "We are going to die!"

Maybe Satan has convinced you that you are going to die. He may have persuaded you that you will never be able to get another job. He might have told you that you will never be healed of that disease. You might think you will never be able to shake that depression. Maybe you are convinced that you will never be able to do anything you really want to do.

You might be asking God, "Well, God, are You going to leave me this way?"

Jesus Spoke the Word

When those disciples woke Jesus by crying out that they were about to die, He stood in the power of the Holy Ghost. The Scripture says:

> **And he arose, and rebuked the wind, and said unto the sea, Peace, be still. And the wind ceased, and there was a great calm.**
>
> **Mark 4:39**

The Son of the Living God did two things:

First, He spoke to the wind, which had been kicking up the waves, and said, **Peace, be still.** Jesus was not operating as the Son of God but as the Son of Man, anointed by the Holy Ghost.

Then He spoke to the men in the boat:

> **And he said unto them, Why are ye so fearful? how is it that ye have no faith?**
>
> **Mark 4:40**

He was saying to them, "How is it that you don't have faith, that you don't understand who you are or Who I am?"

They had forgotten Who He was and who they were in Him.

Jesus expected Peter, at least, to stand up in the bow of that boat and proclaim, "The Son of the Living God has told us we are going to the other side, so we *are* going to the other side! Now, peace, be still!"

What would have happened if Peter or John or any other disciple had made that statement of faith? The same as when Jesus said it: the winds would have ceased blowing and the waves would have been stilled.

But it requires some revelation for that to happen in the middle of a storm, in the middle of the problem. It requires revelation that the gates of hell shall not prevail, as we read in Matthew's gospel.

You Can Have That Peace in the Midst of the Storm

God did not intend for you to stumble and fall. But if you are not living holy, you *will* stumble and fall. If you do not add to your faith, you *will* stumble and you *will* fall. Even though you might confess and say, "Greater is He that's in me than he that's in the world," you will still stumble and fall — if you don't add those other ingredients to your faith.

But by adding them to your faith, you will get a true revelation of Jesus. Receiving that revelation of Jesus and knowing what He has put inside you brings about security in the midst of the storm. You will be able to sleep on a pillow and keep riding those waves, just like Jesus did.

People may say to you, "Don't you really know or understand what's happening? Don't you care?"

But you will be able to stand firm against the wiles of the devil that try to bring you down off that rock of revelation knowledge.

How is it that God could say you would *never* stumble or fall? What does that really mean?

You cannot do that in the flesh, with your own natural knowledge of Jesus. It takes the Holy Ghost to reveal it to you.

The Holy Ghost does not operate where there is sin. He cannot reveal much to you when you are just stumbling and fumbling around.

Some people ask, "How is it that So-and-so can receive something from God when it doesn't seem to happen for me?"

Because that person has received more revelation than you. Even though he may have been in church a shorter length of time than you, maybe he has made himself available to receive more revelation of Jesus. He is seeing Jesus in a brighter light.

This happens more and more as we are open to receiving the true knowledge of Him that has called us to glory and virtue. The big prize is getting the knowledge of Jesus. By seeking Him we will begin to see Him brighter and brighter.

The Holy Spirit wants to show you Jesus in such a way that it really touches your life. Then you will never be the same!

5

Spiritual Intelligence

As we have found in Scripture, there are seven character traits which are to be added to our faith. I want to look closer at one of these characteristics: knowledge. Peter said:

And...giving all diligence, add to your faith virtue; and to virtue *knowledge*.

2 Peter 1:5

We saw before that in this verse the Greek word for "knowledge" is *gnosis*. This knowledge does not mean educational intelligence or experience. It is *spiritual* intelligence.

Spiritual Intelligence in Paul

The apostle Paul operated in this spiritual intelligence throughout his ministry.

In Acts, chapter 27, when he was sailing for Rome, we find him facing rough seas in a time of trouble. On this voyage, he received some inside intelligence from the Holy Ghost. Let's look at this situation.

Now when much time was spent, and when sailing was now dangerous...Paul admonished them,

And said unto them, Sirs, I perceive that this voyage will be with hurt and much damage, not only of the lading and ship, but also of our lives.

Acts 27:9,10

In this instance, we see spiritual intelligence being added to Paul's faith.

Faith without intelligence is blind.

An example of this is an automobile being driven on a mountain road. That vehicle can be moving under much power; but if the driver has no idea where he is going and cannot see around the next bend, the car could crash and burn.

The Tempestuous Storm Came

Paul received spiritual intelligence about the rest of the trip. He warned the men on the ship, but they did not listen.

They continued on with their journey and, as a result, sailed into some rough seas. Scripture tells us about the kind of wind they had to face. It says:

> ...there arose against it a tempestuous wind, called Euroclydon.
>
> **Acts 27:14**

In the Middle East a Euroclydon is a gust of wind that comes from nowhere. Winds on the Red Sea can be calm when all of the sudden a Euroclydon comes out of the northeast. Captains in that region of the world are fearful when a Euroclydon approaches. The winds suddenly get stronger, the waves rise up, and many ships are sunk as the result.

Just as Paul had learned what would happen by receiving spiritual intelligence before their journey, their ship ran into some rough waters:

> And when the ship was caught and was unable to head against the wind, we gave up and letting her drift were borne along.
>
> **Acts 27:16** AMP

This is what happens when you are not listening to God and following His spiritual intelligence. You may want to go in a certain direction, but circumstances will take you in the opposite direction. You will be caught helpless unless you receive some more intelligence.

What happened when the ship was caught in the middle of that Euroclydon? Paul began to seek for more intelligence from the Lord.

Even though in our situation we may have failed to listen to God the first time, God will keep on working with us because He loves us. He knows how we can be hardheaded, thickheaded, brick-headed, bullheaded — just downright stupid. (And I'm pointing a finger at myself, too.) God knows how we are. Sometimes our head can be as hard as a piece of wood, but God keeps working with us.

And we being exceedingly tossed with a tempest, the next day they lightened the ship.

Acts 27:18

That ship was hit so hard by the storm that those men had to lighten their load, so they threw out all of their cargo. They would not have lost their cargo had they listened to the Lord speaking to them through His servant, Paul.

God does not want you to lose your possessions, but you *will* lose them if you are too hardheaded to listen to His instructions and heed His directions.

That storm raged on against the ship for fourteen days. Can you imagine being caught in a Euroclydon for fourteen days?

"Be of Good Cheer!"

In the midst of this storm, Paul received some more intelligence:

But after long abstinence Paul stood forth in the midst of them, and said, Sirs, ye should have hearkened unto me, and not have loosed from Crete, and to have gained this harm and loss.

And now I exhort you to be of good cheer....

Acts 27:21,22

Though caught in that violent wind, in the midst of that Euroclydon, in the middle of all those winds and waves, the men were told, **Be of good cheer.** They could have been dead at any moment. Had they capsized, nobody would have ever found them. Even if they had sent out a distress call, they could never have been reached in time.

But they were told by Paul to:

> ...be of good cheer: for there shall be no loss of any man's life among you, but of the ship.
>
> **Acts 27:22**

God was saying to them through Paul, "You are going to forfeit the ship because you did not listen, but your lives will be saved. So be of good cheer — having your life is more important than anything else."

Notice what Paul said in verse 23:

> For there stood by me this night the angel of God, whose I am, and whom I serve.

This happened long after Paul had sought God.

Today we want God to answer us all the time. We want Him to answer us every moment, instantly. But it does not always come that way.

Some days you will have to spend time in fasting and prayer, seeking God on your knees — for days, sometimes for weeks, sometimes for months — to find out what God wants to do.

"Fear Not!"

Paul shared with those sailors some inside intelligence. He said:

> For there stood by me this night the angel of God, whose I am, and whom I serve,
>
> Saying, [inside intelligence:] Fear not, Paul; thou must be brought before Caesar: and, lo, God hath given thee all them that sail with thee.
>
> **Acts 27:23,24**

He was telling them, "Everybody aboard this ship will be saved." He said:

> **Wherefore, sirs, be of good cheer: for I believe God, that it shall be even as it was told me.**
>
> **Acts 27:25**

Think about that: **It shall be even as it was told me.** How exciting!

That's the way it will be when God tells you something. Just make sure it is really God that has told you. When God tells you, then it *will* be that way!

So you can be of good cheer, even in the midst of life's great storm — whether cancer, family problems, financial difficulties, job trouble or some other problem area. Some "great Euroclydon" may come into your life, but you can be of good cheer. The God Whom you serve will save you in the midst of that storm. He will save you even when you are caught out in the darkness. He will save you even in the midst of your problem — whatever it may be.

"Stay in the Boat!"

> **Then fearing lest we should have fallen upon rocks, they [the shipmen] cast four anchors out of the stern, and wished for the day.**
>
> **And as the shipmen were about to flee out of the ship, when they had let down the boat into the sea, under colour as though they would have cast anchors out of the foreship,**
>
> **Paul said to the centurion and to the soldiers, Except these abide in the ship, ye cannot be saved.**
>
> **Acts 27:29-31**

The sailors were ready to jump ship once they got close to the land. They were ready to try to swim ashore. But Paul was given some more inside intelligence. He was saying to them, "If you get out of this boat, you won't make it."

God was saying, "I will save you, but you have to stay in the boat."

There is a time to get out of the boat and walk on the water, but there is also a time to stay out of the water and in the boat.

Paul was saying to those sailors, "Unless you stay in this boat, you cannot be saved."

This time they all listened to him!

Be Filled With Peace

> **And while the day was coming on, Paul besought them all to take meat, saying, This day is the fourteenth day that ye have tarried and continued fasting, having taken nothing.**
>
> **Wherefore I pray you to take some meat: for this is for your health: for there shall not be an hair fall from the head of any of you.**
>
> **Acts 27:33,34**

In the midst of the Euroclydon, Paul told the men to sit down and have something to eat. He was saying, "Let's take care of ourselves even while this boat is rocking."

That sounded like Jesus, as we read in Mark's gospel, chapter 4. When He and His disciples got in the boat, He told them to go to the other side; then He went to sleep on a pillow. When that storm came, they were so afraid that they had to wake Him up. Jesus could sleep through the storm because He was filled with peace. He had those seven characteristics, as we have read in Second Peter, chapter 1.

When you have those seven characteristics and find yourself in the midst of a Euroclydon, you can know that same peace Jesus knew, even when everybody around you is panicking. You can sleep when nobody else can. You can rejoice when nobody else can. That's because you have inside intelligence that the Lord is on your side, no matter what may be going on around you.

Through all that storm, the apostle Paul had that same kind of peace, and he was able to share that peace with those sailors. Because they listened to him, they eventually made it to shore.

The Bible does not tell us this, but I would imagine that when they got to shore, they kneeled down and kissed the ground. Instead of doing that though, they should have lifted their hands to the Lord and said: "Lord, thank You for that inside intelligence. Forgive us for not listening. We lost our ship and our cargo, but You saved us anyway because You had a vessel we should listen to."

Give No Place to the Devil

After they had taken shelter on an island, we see something else happening to Paul:

> And when Paul had gathered a bundle of sticks, and laid them on the fire, there came a viper out of the heat, and fastened on his hand.
>
> **Acts 28:3**

When that dangerous viper grabbed onto Paul's hand, the natives who saw it thought he must have done something wrong and deserved to die. But Paul gave it no serious attention. It says:

> And he shook off the beast into the fire, and felt no harm.
>
> **Acts 28:5**

The barbarians just watched him, waiting for him to die:

> Howbeit they looked when he should have swollen, or fallen down dead suddenly: but after they had looked a great while, and saw no harm come to him, they changed their minds, and said that he was a god.
>
> **Acts 28:6**

Paul just kept acting normally because he already had inside information. He knew that God, as his Protector, was all he needed.

Receive From God

You receive inside information like that once you have come to know Who Jesus really is and allow those seven characteristics to be added to your life.

By spending more time on your face seeking the Lord, nothing — I said *nothing!* — will stop you from receiving from God.

Then you will not be blind to the ways of God. You will never stumble or fall when your eyes are on Him. You will not forget what has been revealed to you. The Holy Ghost will give you that revelation.

Once you have received that inside intelligence, you can go on regardless of what may be happening around you.

6
Put On Your Spiritual Track Shoes

> And beside this, *giving all diligence*, add to your faith.
>
> 2 Peter 1:5

> ...*adding your diligence* [to the divine promises], employ every effort in exercising your faith.
>
> 2 Peter 1:5 AMP

As you have been reading through the pages of this book, I believe the Holy Spirit has revealed some things to you that can — and should — revolutionize your life. If you have an ear to hear and have been hearing what the Holy Ghost is saying, your Christian walk should have begun to make a change. I believe He has been saying some things vital for this hour.

We read in Second Peter, chapter 1, that you are to **give diligence to make your calling and election sure, for *if ye do these things*, ye shall never fall** (v. 10). *These things*, as Peter had listed in verses 5-7, are to be added to your faith. As we read in verse 4, God has made a way for us to escape the corruption that is in the world through lust.

In today's world, corruption has brought about depravity. There is an inordinately strong desire in mankind for the things of this world. More than ever before, we are seeing people filled with lust of the flesh, lust of the eyes and pride of life. In addition, we have watched people become consumed with the love of money, which Scripture says is the root cause of all evil. (1 Tim. 6:10.)

Mankind has become depraved to such an extent that in many ways we have seen our great nation fall away from its foundation principles. God has been shut out of schools and removed from public policies. The Church of the Lord Jesus Christ has been attacked as the hordes of Satan have been unleashed into this nation. As a result, we are seeing the breakup of the family, the rise of crime and the collapse of this nation's economy. These results are based more upon what has happened spiritually than what has been done naturally. People have turned from Almighty God.

We are seeing the depravity of Satan's attack upon our country, because this nation has been the lighthouse of the world. Cities, in particular, are feeling the brunt of this assault. It's a fact that in our cities people go to church more than anywhere else. Satan knows that, so he wants to attack and wipe out those who are spending more time in the house of God.

But this country can be restored!

The Finest Hour!

The only way this will happen, however, is when the Church of the Lord Jesus Christ decides to no longer be caught up in the world's corruption. We must consider the calling of God and the work of the Lord to be more important and more valuable than the things of this world.

As God's people, we must be willing to win the lost by getting the Word of the Lord out into the world and bringing people into the Kingdom. We must consider God's ways to be more important than the jobs we hold, the vacations we take, the fine homes we have — more important than anything else in our lives!

The Church of the Lord Jesus Christ must become single-minded.

The Church must understand that it is called and anointed by God for a mission, that this mission is coming close to its finest hour, that this mission requires diligence.

We must be diligent to add to our faith those seven characteristics we discussed from Second Peter 1:5-7.

God is saying throughout the Church, "Church, I don't want you to stumble anymore. I don't want you to fall down again."

The Lord is getting His Church ready for its finest hour. He is preparing us for the time when things will get worse and worse in the natural realm.

In chapter 24 of Matthew's gospel, Jesus told us that when summer is nigh we can look for the return of the Lord. (v. 32.) That "season" in the Bible began May 14, 1948, when Israel returned to its homeland and became a nation again. The summer has come!

God's Wrath Against Sin

Jesus said there would be wars and rumors of wars, earthquakes and an abundance of them, and many more occurrences of natural disasters. That means men and women all over the world will become more depraved, seeking more things of the flesh.

In the first chapter of the book of Romans, we see the apostle Paul describing the wrath of God coming against sin:

> **For the wrath of God is revealed from heaven against all ungodliness and unrighteousness of men, who hold the truth in unrighteousness;**
>
> **...when they knew God, they glorified him not as God, neither were thankful; but became vain in their imaginations, and their foolish heart was darkened.**
>
> **Wherefore God also gave them up to uncleanness through the lusts of their own hearts, to dishonour their own bodies between themselves:**
>
> **Who changed the truth of God into a lie, and worshipped and served the creature more than the Creator, who is blessed for ever. Amen.**

For this cause God gave them up unto vile affections: for even their women did change the natural use into that which is against nature:

And likewise also the men, leaving the natural use of the woman, burned in their lust one toward another; men with men working that which is unseemly, and receiving in themselves that recompence of their error which was meet.

Romans 1:18,21,24-27

More and more these days, mankind is going after the flesh — men lying with men, women lying with women, babies by the millions losing their lives through abortion. The world today is continually moving further and further away from God's truth.

The Glorious Church!

The enemy shall come in more and more like a flood against the remnant of the Church that has decided to add to its faith, diligently making its calling and election sure, esteeming the things of God more highly than the things of this world.

This part of God's people will be spending more time in prayer and fasting. They will be listening to the Holy Ghost and obeying His voice.

When He tells them to be a witness in their community, sharing Jesus with others in their neighborhood and on their job, they will be obedient.

When He says to go across town and visit with someone, they will follow His instructions.

When He says to call a friend on the phone and minister to that person, they will do it.

When He says to spend time in intercessory prayer, praying for the world, for the nations, for the lost, they will be quick to obey.

That Church is the glorious Church!

When the enemy comes in like a flood against the rest of the world, the Spirit of the Lord will raise up a standard against him. (Isa. 59:19.) That "standard" will be the Church of the Lord Jesus Christ flowing in the power and anointing of the Holy Spirit. The Church will be used by God like never before.

Looking Through Spiritual Eyes

Satan will try to divide the Church and get us to turn inwardly on each other. He will try to stop the anointing that has already begun. He knows how the Holy Ghost will not manifest His anointing within a strife-filled situation.

Satan knows his time is short, so he is working overtime to stop the Church. All kinds of things are being thrown in our path to try to hurt us and get us out of the way. But because we have seen Jesus, we are able to escape the corruption in the world and all its destruction. We can appropriate the promises of God so that we will neither stumble nor fall.

God, through the Holy Ghost in your life, will cause you to avoid the various obstacles Satan has set before you. You will see them not in the natural but with your spiritual eye. Then you will know inside yourself whether to move to the right or to the left, to go over or under. Jesus will be living big inside you!

People will say, "You can't go into that place; things there are too tough to deal with."

But the Lord will say, "You have the Greater One inside you, and greater is He that is in you than he that is in the world."

Do you believe that? If for some reason you don't, I want to point out another verse of Scripture which says:

> **Herein is our love made perfect, that we may have boldness in the day of judgment....**
>
>

1 John 4:17

This day of judgment is not when you stand before God. The day of judgment is when you face the temptations, tests, trials that Satan throws against you in this world. You can have boldness in that day of judgment. Why? The verse continues:

> **...because as he is, so are we in this world.**

"As He Is, So Are We!"

Think about that: **As he is, so are we.**

Let me ask you this: how is Jesus now?

Is He sick? No!

Is He fearful? No!

Is He defeated by the devil? No!

Jesus is victorious!

And *as He is* — strong, courageous, victorious — so can you be in this world as you are flowing in the power of the Holy Spirit. Satan has no power over you, the believer. When people see you, they will see Jesus! Instead of always stumbling or falling, you can be walking just like Jesus walked: in the power and anointing of Almighty God.

Satan worked hard trying to make Jesus stumble and fall when He was here on the earth. He wanted Jesus to strike out in the flesh, but it didn't work. Jesus *did* strike, but not in the way Satan wanted. Jesus went after His real enemy, but He did it in the spirit, performing miracle after miracle after miracle. He laid hands on the sick, having compassion on the people and ministering unto them; and He supernaturally fed thousands of men, women and children. (Matt. 14:14,21.)

That's the way it will be as you receive more revelation of Jesus. You will be able to act just like He did. If you or somebody near you is hurt, you will react in the spirit instead of the flesh, punching out Satan instead of another person.

Be in a Hurry for God!

As we have read several times in Second Peter 1:5, it says, **Giving all diligence, add to your faith**; then it follows with the seven characteristics to be added to our faith. God wants us as His Church to be diligent to add those qualities to our faith.

The Greek word for *diligence* means earnestness and haste.[1] That means we are to add those characteristics to our faith, and to do it diligently.

Then in Second Peter 1:10, the word *diligence* is mentioned again. It says:

Wherefore the rather, brethren, give diligence.

This word *diligence* also means to give earnestness, to be in haste; or in other words, to have great zeal.

The time has come for us to get in a hurry to do the things God desires for us to do. What happens will happen quickly.

In comparison, think how time seems to be going faster these days. What once would have taken decades has taken only a few years. What took years now takes only months; and months, only weeks; and weeks, only days; and days, only hours.

Things have been speeded up. It's now time for us to get in haste, to put on our spiritual track shoes. The Lord has laid out a plan, and we must be in a hurry to get it done. We must cut things short and get right to God's work, doing it in a hurry, because we no longer have much time.

---

[1]Strong, "Greek Dictionary of the New Testament," p. 66, #4710.

The Harvest Time Is Coming!

Let's look in Proverbs, chapter 10:

He becometh poor that dealeth with a slack hand: but the hand of the diligent maketh rich.

He that gathereth in summer is a wise son: but he that sleepeth in harvest is a son that causeth shame.

Proverbs 10:4,5

The harvest time is coming! Millions and billions of people will be ripe to receive the Gospel. They will be ripe to grow from the infantile, babyhood state in Christendom to spiritual adulthood in Him, casting aside all the things of the flesh.

The things people fight about and worry about so much do not really matter once they turn their lives over to Almighty God. All that matters to them then is doing what God wants done in this day and hour.

Diligently Abound in Him

Remember Peter said, **If these things be in you, *and abound*, they make you that ye shall neither be barren nor unfruitful in the knowledge of our Lord Jesus Christ** (2 Peter 1:8). By abounding in all those seven things he listed earlier, you will have the full and exact knowledge of Jesus.

Look at Second Corinthians 8:7:

Therefore, *as ye abound* in every thing, in faith, and utterance, and knowledge, and in all diligence, and in your love to us, *see that ye abound* in this grace also.

You are to grow in diligence — in earnestness, in zeal, in haste. But being diligent and hasty is a value judgment. That's when you make a decision about what is important.

When some merchandise you want has gone on sale, that sale may only last for a few hours. There is a deadline. You have to get to that store before all the merchandise is sold. That's when you become diligent and hasty. You might even put off a meal for a while. There may be only a few items left on the shelf at that price, so you make a beeline straight to the store.

You need to be just as diligent now regarding the things of God. The "sale" is about to end. There is enough "merchandise" for everybody, but the Word of God tells us only a few will be diligent to take advantage of it. Jesus said:

> **Enter ye in at the strait gate: for wide is the gate, and broad is the way, that leadeth to destruction, and many there be which go in thereat:**
>
> **Because strait is the gate, and narrow is the way, which leadeth unto life, and few there be that find it.**
> **Matthew 7:13,14**

There will be those who decide to get in line in a hurry. They will make a beeline to God, forgetting about everything else. They will want to do the work of the Lord.

Be Diligent To Do God's Work

As Paul said, we are to abound in all diligence. So shake yourself! Get up and start moving in a hurry! Stop lying in "Delilah's lap," allowing your head to be stroked by the world, feeling good because everything is okay with you right now.

Things might be okay with *you*, but is everything in your life okay with God?

God sees a world of people who need His Word, who need to find what you have found in Jesus. He sees a nation of people who are being defeated, not because of the Japanese or Germans but because the people no longer really know Who Jesus is. God wants those who know the Truth, who have been called to share that Truth with others, to begin being diligent about doing His work right now.

Be Diligent To Do God's Will

The hand of the diligent shall bear rule: but the slothful shall be under tribute.

Proverbs 12:24

The diligent are the ones who ride the high place. Now there will be saints of God who are riding the low place and living beneath their privileges, but that is not because it is the will of God.

The will of God is not automatic. He has given believers a choice. They can decide for themselves what they want to do. They can add to their faith, or they can leave it out. They can make their calling and election sure, or they can be casualties on the road to perdition. That choice rests in the hand of every believer.

The time is over for you to be living as close to the world as you can and still be trying to receive God's pleasure. If you are always walking close to the world's edge, just watch out — you will soon fall back into sin.

The people who are riding in the high places with God will be eager to know His perfect will for them and walk in it. They will want to be flowing in the power of the Holy Ghost, and all those worldly things will not matter anymore.

Laziness Opens the Door for Satan

The slothful [or lazy] man roasteth not that which he took in hunting: but the substance of a diligent man is precious.

Proverbs 12:27

The lazy man will not get the chance to partake of that which belongs to him. Because of his laziness, doors will be opened for the enemy to steal from him that which God has provided.

The time is gone for us to allow Satan to run over us and steal from us. We cannot be permitting him to win over the Church of the Lord Jesus Christ.

The time has come for the Church to take its rightful place as the army of God filled with the greatest weaponry ever known to man. God's army will move back the gates of hell and take away all the enemy's wares. Those possessions were not really his to begin with; they belonged to God. Everything belongs to our heavenly Father, so it is time for the Church to take back what belongs to it!

Now by "possessions" I do not mean material things, like gold and cattle (although they really do belong to God); I am referring to what really counts to God: men, women and children. They belong to Him.

> How then shall they call on him in whom they have not believed? and how shall they believe in him of whom they have not heard? and how shall they hear without a preacher?
>
> And how shall they preach, except they be sent? as it is written, How beautiful are the feet of them that preach the gospel of peace, and bring glad tidings of good things!
>
> **Romans 10:14,15**

How can people hear without a preacher?

How can they believe on Jesus if they have not heard about Him?

How can they accept Him in Whom they have not believed?

God is calling us to use our faith to win others. He is calling us to spend time in intercessory prayer and break the power of the enemy — over our families, our churches, our cities, our nation. Through intercessory prayer, we will be allowing the power of the Holy Ghost to work through us as we travail in the Spirit of Almighty God.

The Diligent Receives From God

**The soul of the sluggard desireth, and hath nothing:
but the soul of the diligent shall be made fat.**

Proverbs 13:4

The soul of a lazy person wants everything he sees and everything others have.

You might say, "I want to flow in the Spirit and have the love of God flowing through me." But it will not happen unless you are diligent to receive what God has for you. You have to take the proper time and make sure you add those seven characteristics to your faith.

The soul of the diligent shall have everything that belongs to him, everything God has promised: protection, resources, anointing, vision by the Holy Ghost, knowledge — exact knowledge — of the Lord.

The time is coming when hearing from God will be the discerning point between making it and not making it. It may not be in a week, a month, a year or even a decade, but that time is coming in our lifetime.

The Spirit of the Lord is warning the Church of the Lord Jesus Christ about all that is coming. He is spreading this message all around. He has taught us about faith so that we will be able to take the shield of faith and stand. And He is turning up the anointing, which breaks every yoke. (Isa. 10:27.) However, His anointing can only be entrusted to people who meet the conditions given in Second Peter, chapter 1.

7

Pay Attention to This!

Peter's second letter was written to those who have received like precious faith. That's us! As believers in Jesus Christ, we have received like precious faith through the righteousness of God in Jesus our Lord.

Grace and peace has been multiplied to us through the knowledge of God and of Jesus.

Again, the seven character traits listed, which we should be diligently adding to our faith, are:

- virtue — moral excellence
- knowledge — spiritual intelligence
- temperance — self-control
- patience — steadfastness
- godliness — holiness
- brotherly kindness or affection
- the love of God

These characteristics must be in the bloom of every Christian.

When these character traits are abounding in us, we will **neither be barren nor unfruitful in the knowledge of our Lord Jesus Christ** (v. 8).

Then we will not be blind spiritually. We will be able to see afar off and know we have victory over our old sins. When Satan tries to bring one of them back on us, we can say, "No! I won't receive it! I already have victory over that in Jesus' name!"

Through the knowledge of what Jesus has provided for us, and our acceptance of His work on the cross, we have been placed in the position where we will never have to stumble or fall again!

"Pay Attention Now!"

Let's look at some more words Peter had to say to the Church:

> **Wherefore I will not be negligent to** *put you always in remembrance* **of these things, though ye know them, and be established in the present truth.**
>
> **Yea, I think it meet, as long as I am in this tabernacle, to** *stir you up by putting you in remembrance;*
>
> **Knowing that shortly I must put off this my tabernacle, even as our Lord Jesus Christ hath shewed me.**
>
> **Moreover I will endeavour that ye may be able after my decease to have these things always in remembrance.**
>
> **For we have not followed cunningly devised fables, when we made known unto you the power and coming of our Lord Jesus Christ, but were eyewitnesses of his majesty.**
>
> **2 Peter 1:12-16**

Peter had to stir up the Church by putting them in remembrance of some things. He was saying to them: "I will soon go to be with the Lord. But I want you to know, the things I am telling you are not cunningly devised fables. I heard them with my own ears and saw them with my own eyes."

He goes on further in this chapter to say:

> **We have also a more sure word of prophecy; whereunto ye do well that ye take heed, as unto a light**

that shineth in a dark place, until the day dawn, and the day star arise in your hearts.

2 Peter 1:19

He was saying to the Church:

"You would do well to heed what I have said. Fasten your eyes upon these things. Perk up your ears and listen to what I am saying. Pay much attention, until the morning time comes and drives away all the darkness, until the Daystar — the Son of the light of the Word of God — rises in your heart. Then all that darkness — all ignorance, fears, worries, anything Satan tries to bring against you — will be driven away."

He was telling God's people to pay attention to these things, because, as verse 10 AMP says, ...**if you do this you will** *never stumble or fall.* This is why he was telling us to be in remembrance of these things.

Three Things That Could Happen

After listing those seven ingredients for success in this life, Peter mentions three very important things that could happen if we fail to listen and add those ingredients to our faith. In verse 9 he gives three areas, in particular, where we could stumble or fall. He writes:

But he that lacketh these things [#1] *is blind,* **and [#2]** *cannot see afar off,* **and [#3]** *hath forgotten that he was purged from his old sins.*

2 Peter 1:9

#1: "You Are Blind!"

Blind men fall in the ditch. They stumble over things right in front of them.

If you have no spiritual vision, you will be unable to see what Satan is attempting to do in your life. You will be blind spiritually because you have not added character to your faith.

Though you may be believing God to blow down mountains, you can still act immorally. You may not have spiritual intelligence. You may not be patiently waiting until the right time before acting. You may not be living holy before God. You may not be operating in the love of God.

All these things must be added to keep you from being blind as a bat spiritually. You can be regularly attending a Word church, getting fat on all the Word of God being preached, and still be blind as a bat spiritually by not having added those seven characteristics to your faith.

Spiritual blindness is one of the reasons people get slapped down and stumble and fall. They cannot see because they have not allowed those things to be added to their faith. Peter said, "Pay attention to this!"

#2: "You Can't See Afar Off!"

Not only will you be unable to see what is right in front of you, you will be unable to see what is coming in the future.

God is not in the business of allowing Satan to sneak up behind you and clobber you. Because He can see Satan coming at you a long way off, He wants you to know it, too.

He desires for you to know, to some extent, His plan for your life. But you cannot see it, perceive it, know it and get the benefit of it if you have not added those characteristics to your faith. You may have two or three of them, but you really need all seven to operate in high gear.

Those characteristics don't grow on trees. They must be developed over time. This is a lifework for you. Don't be a Word-taught Christian who is fat in the spirit, yet still carnal.

#3: "But You Were Purged From Your Old Sins!"

If you forget that you have been purged from your old sins, the things you used to do can easily sneak back on you.

You will forget that you have victory over the flesh.

You will forget that you have victory over sin.

You will forget that you have victory over the devil.

It will be just as though you were not even born again. You will look like the world, talk like the world and fall into all kinds of sin — just like the world.

You will have forgotten who you are and where you came from. You will not be able to see the difference between yourself and the world, even though you have been born again and have known the power of the Holy Ghost.

For too long, we have slipped and fallen. God is tired of it. The Church of the Lord Jesus Christ must get its act together. We must begin to make a distinguishing difference between us and the world. We have no business looking and acting like everyone else in the world.

If you really want to be like the world — always drinking, cussing, dancing and finding sex wherever you can — then why stay in church? You are being a stumbling block to all the young Christians in the house of God who see you acting like the world.

You have no business doing anything like the world. You need to operate in the power of Almighty God. But you can only do that through His anointing by acting upon His holy Word and making a decision that you are going to be different from the world.

That does not come by sitting in church and saying amen to your pastor. It comes by making a decision to order your life that way. You have to begin to talk and walk the line, in accordance with the Word of God.

It makes no difference whether you wear a clergy collar or have earned a college degree. God is requiring some things of His people today. He wants us to operate in a higher level of His anointing and power.

There Is a Higher Level!

God is moving! The wind of the Lord is beginning to blow! It is a holiness blow. That move of the Holy Ghost has begun, and His Church is being moved to a higher level. The time has come when we must be listening to what He is saying.

The Lord has been sending me throughout the United States to preach His Word to the Body of Christ. Everywhere I go, I have been sharing the message He has given me and telling the Church that the time is now.

For us to reach that higher level, we must begin to walk in the seven characteristics of God we have discussed in this book. We must have moral excellence, develop self-control, be kind to others and live godly before Him. We must be full of His love. We must have the spiritual intelligence to know what God wants us to do — and then do it!

You were not put in this world just to eat, drink and be merry, so that you can have a good time before you die. God does not care about you having a good time. He put you on this earth to do a job for Him in this hour.

People are going to hell by the millions, and they need to hear the gospel of Jesus Christ. But that will not happen if you live like the world, act like the world and talk like the world. The Bible says judgment begins at the house of God. (1 Peter 4:17.)

You have to make some decisions in your life. You cannot be living like the devil and think you will automatically get to heaven. There is a hell and it is hot! It was not intended for people; it is for the devil. (Rev. 20:10.) But those who are following the devil will go there, too!

You cannot preach Mark 11:23 and believe only that Scripture. You should also read the book of Revelation. It says hell and death will be thrown in the lake of fire. (Rev. 20:14.)

Peter was saying to the Church, "Put these things in your memory and then act upon them."

As we have read in verse 10, he says, **Wherefore the rather, brethren, give diligence....** Diligence is not casualness. It is not moving at your own leisurely pace. He continues: **...give diligence to make your calling and election sure.**

We are not playing games. This is serious business — deadly business. It is eternal business.

8

It's Time to Go On With God!

Follow God's Directions

It's time to hear what God is saying today. Spend time talking to Him, then listen to the Holy Ghost. With the *epignosis* — the exact knowledge of Jesus — you can follow the Holy Ghost like a road map. Concentrate on Him and let Him minister to your spirit.

When He says in your heart, "Don't move," then do what He says and stay right where you are!

When He says, "Move," it may look as though things are in your way, but just pick up your feet and move! You should be ready to go whenever the Holy Ghost gives you instructions.

You receive direction when there is a tugging in your spirit by the Spirit of God. With that tug you hear words like, "Go over that way, and when you get there, do this...."

You might ask, "But, Lord, shouldn't I stay here? Why do You want me over there?"

But the Lord is saying, "I want you to go where I tell you to go, then wait until I tell you what to do next. I'm the Captain; you are to follow orders."

As long as you follow God's orders, you will win in the time of the battle. Whenever you are obedient to His direction, you will never stumble or fall.

By not listening to your Captain and being quick to obey His commands, even when you cannot see what is going on, you could be shot down. You might find yourself in the wrong place at the wrong time.

I would rather have the anointing of the Holy Ghost than anything else I know about in this world. I have learned how valuable the anointing is.

Walk in God's Perfect Will

It's time to make sure you are walking and living in the perfect will of God.

You will be led by the Holy Ghost more and more as the ingredients we found in Second Peter, chapter 1, are added to your life. Then you can watch the power of the Holy Ghost become stronger as the revelation of these truths becomes greater. The sense of joy and peace in God will take you up to that higher spiritual plain.

You will begin to think more about the Lord, concerning yourself with things above, not with things of this earth.

You will say, "Lord, I want to know Your will for me now. I will do what You want me to do, go where You want me to go and do whatever You want me to do."

Then you will see Jesus shining brighter as you see more of Him inside you.

Produce Fruit for God

It's time to be producing the kind of fruit in your life that God is calling for.

Every morning you should ask, "Lord, what do You want me to do today? Where do You want me to go? Who do You want me to witness to?"

Your life must be a witness to every person you know. You must tell people the story that Jesus saves, Jesus lives and Jesus will change their lives too, making a difference in them. By seeing Jesus in you, they will want Him too. As you bring them into the family of God, He will receive glory.

Satan will attempt to keep the person you are to witness to from crossing your path that day. So each morning you need to use your faith and believe God that the wall Satan tries to put between you and that person will be torn down. Then both of you will be where God intends for you to be.

Before boarding an airplane, I believe God for just the right person to be sitting next to me, someone I am to witness to on the trip. For two and a half hours, that person will be trapped. With no place to go, he will get to hear about Jesus and what He has done for me.

God wants to use His Church — everyone, not just the pastors — to share Jesus with people everywhere. He expects those sitting in the pews to begin pastoring the ones who have accepted Jesus as their Lord. That means looking out for them, praying for them, helping them learn for themselves how to stand on God's Word.

After you have led someone to the Lord, God does not want you to stop there; He wants you to attach yourself to that person and begin to feed him or her the Word of God.

Really Commit Your Life to Jesus

Begin to see who you really are and Who is living on the inside of you. His name is Jesus. He is the Son of God. In Scripture He is called the Alpha and the Omega, the Beginning and the End, the First and the Last. (Rev. 1:8,11.) The Jesus Who is living inside you wants you to walk in His power.

I have seen Jesus in the spirit, and I want to move in Him. So I say to Him with an open heart, "Yes, Lord!" Then I begin moving my spiritual feet to get myself into position in Him.

As a child of God — having received Jesus as your Lord — you need to be sure your life is really committed to Him. If you need to make any changes in your life, do it now! When you were first born again and received the Holy Spirit, you were changed, but there is always more changing to be done.

It's time you make the decision to let loose of all the worldly things. Money and fame don't mean a thing. All that will last is what you do for Christ! He will use you to do His will on the earth.

I want you to receive this message, my friend. I got it straight from the Lord through His Word. He wants you to reach the point where you never have to stumble or fall. But if you do, don't blame God, or your pastor, or your church. Just ask for God's forgiveness right then, and start again.

I can stand before the Lord now and say, "Father, I shared the message You gave me, so Your people know what You expect of them. I believe they will ride on the high places. They will mount up on the wings of eagles; they will run and not be weary; they will walk and not faint.[1] They will flow in the anointing and in the power of Almighty God. And Satan is trembling!"

You see, Satan knows what is coming so he is working feverishly against it. That is why we are seeing things happening like never before in this world. There are some weird and crazy things going on, but we will see even more and more as Satan gets wilder and wilder. But he knows his time is short!

It is like that Friday night after Satan had crucified the Lord. The demons were partying in the pits of hell. But I think Satan may have been a little worried whether Jesus would stay dead. He could remember what had happened

---

[1]Isaiah 40:31.

with Lazarus. Lazarus had been dead four days, but on that fourth day the Lord called out, "Loose him and let him go!" and Lazarus rose up and walked. (John 11:1-44.) So Satan was wondering if death could hold the Lord.

Then came Sunday morning! The Holy Ghost energized Jesus, and He rose from the dead. The stone was rolled away and Jesus, the King of Kings, walked out of that grave!

I'm here to tell you that the Sunday for the Church is on its way. On that Sunday morning the stone of the enemy will be rolled out of our way, and the Church of the Lord Jesus Christ shall rise!

His Church shall rise with the same resurrection power that raised Jesus from the dead. We can walk in that power and have the same effect as when Jesus rose from the grave. The saints who were in the graves came up out of those graves and walked in Jerusalem, appearing to many. (Matt. 27:50-53.)

When the Church of Jesus Christ rises again, those who are in the grave of sin and sickness will rise up out of that grave and follow the members of the Church into the glorious light of Jesus Christ. We will be saved for all eternity!

Are you ready to make a commitment to the Lord?

Maybe you are saved but are as carnal as can be. If so, you need to get right with the Lord. There are blinders over your eyes and you cannot even see in front of you. But God does not want you to stumble; neither does He want you to fall.

It's time for you to let Him burn out the sin in your life. You need to get rid of the waste, becoming cleaned and holy before Almighty God! He wants to change you, to fill you, to make you different. You need to say yes to Him now!

Or maybe you always do good things but have not fully yielded yourself to God. You have not given up your ambitions and taken on His ambitions for you. The Lord is calling you for His service and is requiring commitment from you. He has provided salvation and the Holy Spirit for you, but He is expecting you to serve Him to the fullest extent.

Cry out to Him now and say: "Change me, Lord! I don't want to stumble anymore. I don't want to fall anymore. I want to walk in the straight line with the Holy Ghost. Let me not veer to the right or to the left, but let me go straight on and into Your glory!"

You can watch then as the Lord begins to change you — and you *will* be changed!

So set your faith on Him and say, "Father, I receive it, in the name of Jesus."

I believe He will give you spiritual eyesight and you will be able to see through His eyes — as long as you "stay in the boat."

"Say, *Yes, Lord!*"

Now pray this to your Father in heaven:

"Father, I say, *Yes, Lord*, to Your will.

"As Your servant, I will do what You want me to do, go where You want me to go, say what You want me to say. I will be what You want me to be.

"I will use my talent, my voice, my education for You, Lord. Everything You have given me will be used for You. I am willing to leave behind what the world is offering me and say to You, *Yes, Lord!*"

God wants all of your life right now. Let your education be in God. Let your career be in God. Let the Holy Ghost speak to you and minister to you. Let Him have His way with you. He may be leading you into some new things — a new career, a new school, a new ministry. He may be sending you to places you have never been before.

It's time to humble yourself under the mighty hand of God. It's time that you let go of your pride and submit yourself completely to Him; He will exalt you in due time. (1 Peter 5:6.)

I pray that you have that multiplied grace and peace in your life, that through the knowledge of Jesus you will never stumble or fall. I pray that these things be in you, that they abound in you, that you walk more and more in the revelation of Jesus.

You need to believe God for these things, speaking by faith. After believing you receive, begin to rejoice that it is already done for you in the name of the Lord Jesus of Nazareth. Begin to praise His holy Name. Rejoice in Him and give Him honor.

Now see yourself flowing in that power, that anointing and that holiness in the name of Jesus.

"Stay in His Boat!"

The Word of the Lord to you now is: Stay in His boat. Then you won't be washed away by the storm.

The storm is coming upon the world. It is growing darker by the day. But those who name the Name of the Lord and live in accordance with His Word will be sheltered from the storm.

By staying in the ark of safety you will not be swept away like the people in Noah's day. Noah stood forth as a prophet of God, delivering the message that it was going to rain, but the people would not listen. Because it did not happen immediately, they just laughed and paid no attention. As a result, they all drowned. (See Gen. 6 and 7.)

There is coming upon this world a kind of decadence that people have never seen. But it will not harm you as a child of God. You will be able to go through it...

...*if* you dedicate yourself to God;

...*if* you do what He is saying;

...*if* you live holy before Him;

...*if* you "stay in His boat."

Always remember: God loves you. So allow the power of the Holy Ghost to flow into you and through you. Then you can ride out the storm in this life and walk in the blessings of Almighty God.

God wants your life — *all* of it — dedicated to Him today. The Word of the Lord is for those who will listen. We are not playing games.

So give Him praise and honor and glory now for what He has done and will do for you. Through Him, you will *never* stumble or fall! He is worthy to be praised!

About the Author

Keith Butler is the founder and pastor of Word of Faith Christian Center in Detroit, Michigan, which was begun on January 14, 1979, and now has a congregation of well over 9,000 members. He also pastors Faith Christian Center in Fayetteville, Georgia, which began in August, 1993.

Rev. Butler is a pastor and Bible teacher who ministers in seminars, conventions and churches throughout the country. His ministerial emphasis is on teaching line by line, with instruction on how God's Word can be applied to daily living. His television and radio ministry, "The Living Word," reaches into several states.

Pastor Butler and his lovely wife, Deborah, have three beautiful children: Andre, Michelle and Kristina.

To contact Keith Butler,
write:

Keith Butler
P. O. Box 34546
Detroit, Michigan 48234

Please include your prayer requests and comments when you write.

Additional copies of
this book
are available from your local bookstore.

HARRISON HOUSE
Tulsa, Oklahoma 74153

The Harrison House Vision

Proclaiming the truth and the power
Of the Gospel of Jesus Christ
With excellence;

Challenging Christians to
Live victoriously,
Grow spiritually,
Know God intimately.